G000167721

Best
TEA SHOP WALKS
on
LLEYN & ANGLESEY

Dorothy Hamilton

Published by Sigma Leisure – an imprint of
Sigma Press, 1 South Oak Lane, Wilmslow, Cheshire SK9 6AR, England.

British Library Cataloguing in Publication Data
A CIP record for this book is available from the British Library.

ISBN: 1-85058-724-8

Typesetting and Design by: Sigma Press, Wilmslow, Cheshire

Cover: Coastal path near Porth Dinllaen, Lleyn

Maps: Jeremy Semmens

Photographs: Dorothy Hamilton

Printed by: MFP Design and Print

Disclaimer: the information in this book is given in good faith and is believed to be correct at the time of publication. No responsibility is accepted by either the author or publisher for errors or omissions, or for any loss or injury howsoever caused. Only you can judge your own fitness, competence and experience.

Contents

Introduction   **1**
  The Tea Shops   4
  The Walks   4
  Public Transport   5
  Welsh Place Names   5

The Walks

1. Criccieth   **8**
Distance: 5 miles.

2. Llanystumdwy   **13**
Distance: 3¼ or 6 miles.

3. Pwllheli   **18**
Distance: 3 miles

4. Llanbedrog   **22**
Distance: 5 miles.

5. Abersoch   **27**
Distance: 5¼ miles.

6. Aberdaron   **31**
Distance: 6 miles.

7. Uwchmynydd 37
Distance: 4 miles

8. Whistling Sands 41
Distance: 6½ miles.

9. Llangwnnadl 46
Distance: 6¾ miles.

10. Morfa Nefyn 50
Distance: 5½ miles.

11. Llithfaen 54
Distance: 3 or 5½ miles.

12. Caernarfon 59
Distance: 5¾ miles.

13. Newborough Warren 64
Distance: 3½ miles.

14. Newborough and Llanddwyn Island 68
Distance: 8½ miles.

15. Aberffraw 73
Distance: 4¾ miles.

16. Rhosneigr 77
Distance: 4¾ miles.

17. Trearddur Bay 82
Distance: 6 or 7½ miles.

18. South Stack and Holyhead Mountain   **88**

          Distance: 3 miles.

19. North Stack   **92**

          Distance: 4 miles.

20. Cemaes   **96**

          Distance: 7 miles.

21. Moelfre   **101**

          Distance: 3¾ miles.

22. Benllech   **106**

          Distance: 5½ miles.

23. Red Wharf Bay   **111**

          Distance: 6 miles.

24. Penmon Point   **116**

          Distance: 3 miles.

25. Beaumaris   **121**

          Distance: 2¼ or 5¾ miles.

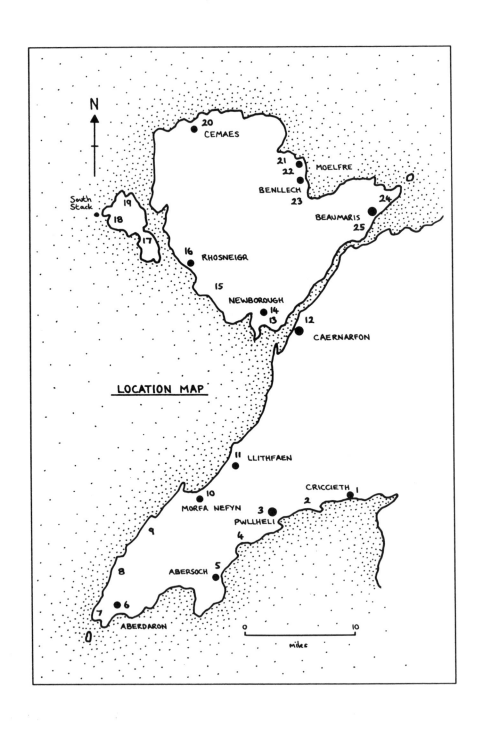

N

LOCATION MAP

20 CEMAES

21
22 MOELFRE
BENLLECH
23

South
Stack
19
18
17

24
BEAUMARIS
25

16 RHOSNEIGR

15

NEWBOROUGH
14
13
12
CAERNARFON

11 LLITHFAEN

CRICCIETH 1
10
MORFA NEFYN
3
2
PWLLHELI
4
9

8
ABERSOCH 5

6
7
ABERDARON
0

0   10
miles

Introduction

The Lleyn peninsula and the island of Anglesey have some of the most varied and beautiful coastal scenery in Wales, from sandy beaches and quiet coves to magnificent high cliffs. Long stretches of both coastlines have been designated Areas of Outstanding Natural Beauty.

Extending west of Snowdonia's mountains, the long arm of Lleyn tapers into the Irish Sea. Reminiscent of Cornwall in shape and position, the peninsula has its own 'Land's End', uncommercialised with spectacular views of Bardsey Island. The north coast has few settlements and many miles of low cliffs looking out to Caernarfon Bay. In contrast, several small resorts lie along the sheltered south coast with its sandy bays.

To the north, Anglesey's varied coastline comprises sandy beaches, tidal estuaries, areas of sand dunes, remote coves and dramatic cliff scenery. From high cliffs on Holy Island a footpath climbs to the summit of Holyhead Mountain, Anglesey's highest summit and an outstanding viewpoint.

Anglesey was part of mainland Wales until the last Ice Age when retreating glaciers melted and flooded the valley that is now the Menai Strait. The bedrock of the island is Pre-Cambrian, visible at South Stack on Holy Island. Melting glaciers left behind a thick blanket of glacial drift and boulder clay, creating fertile soil. During the Middle Ages Anglesey became known as Mon Mam Cymru, Anglesey, Mother of Wales because of the vast quantities of corn that could be grown on the island. Both Anglesey and Lleyn have a much lower annual rainfall than nearby mountainous Snowdonia.

Woodlands are limited in both areas, but the riverside path beside the River Dwyfor at Llanystumdwy and the walk through Newborough Forest should not be missed. Coastal walks are, of course, the main attraction on both Lleyn and Anglesey, and these range from the gentle dunes of Newborough Warren to the high cliffs at the western tip of Lleyn and Holy Island. The rare chough may be seen in both places and thousands of seabirds nest at South Stack. Watch out for seals, especially off Lleyn's north coast. Cliff paths run through colourful gardens of flowers in spring and early summer.

Lleyn and Anglesey have been occupied since the Stone Age. On Mynydd Rhiw near Aberdaron pits mark the site of a Neolithic axe factory. These New Stone Age people built tombs for their dead and several can be seen on Anglesey. There are few remains of the later Bronze Age. About 600 BC, Celtic tribes from continental Europe arrived in Britain, bringing with them knowledge of working iron. They built round huts and established forts on headlands and hilltops. Lleyn and Anglesey have impressive remains from this period. The walk from Moelfre on Anglesey visits the remarkable hut group of Din Lligwy, which was occupied during the Roman era. A magnificent Celtic treasure hoard was found in Llyn Cerrig Bach on Anglesey when a runway was being built at RAF Valley during the Second World War. Swords, spears and chariot wheels had been thrown into the lake as an offering to gods.

After the Roman invasion of southern Britain in AD 43 many Celtic warriors fled to Wales and found refuge in the territory of the Ordovices on Anglesey. At that time it was the main centre of the druids, and in AD 60 the Roman leader Suetonius Paulinus decided to stamp out this source of resistance by attacking the island. While the druids prayed and cursed frantically on the shore a flotilla of flat-bottomed boats ferried the Roman soldiers across the strait. They slaughtered the druids and burnt the sacred groves, ending the old religion. Paulinus and his troops then left Anglesey to deal with a revolt by Queen Boudicca in south-east England. The conquest of the Ordovices of north Wales was finally achieved in AD 77 when Agricola founded a fort at Segontium near Caernarfon. It was garrisoned until the end of the 4th century. A naval base was established at Holyhead in the 3rd century and the Romans built a watch tower on Holyhead Mountain.

When the Romans left Wales, Irish invaders attempted to settle in Anglesey and west Wales. It is believed they were eventually expelled by Cunedda, a Celtic chieftain from northern Britain. In the 6th century an influx of missionaries, mainly from Ireland, reached Wales and the Christian ruler Maelgwn Gwynedd, said to be Cunedda's great grandson, endowed land at Holyhead and Penmon for the building of monasteries. St Cadfan and other Celtic priests from Brittany established a monastery on Bardsey Island, off Lleyn, around AD 516. In the 7th century monks from Bangor Iscoed near Wrexham fled to the island after their monastery was destroyed by the Saxons, and for many centuries afterwards the journey to

Bardsey was a recognised pilgrimage. Three pilgrimages to Bardsey were considered equal to one pilgrimage to Rome.

During this period Vikings who held bases in Dublin and the Isle of Man frequently crossed the Irish Sea to raid Anglesey. Monasteries came under attack and in AD 968 the palace at Aberffraw was partly destroyed. They failed to establish any settlements, but Viking names recall their history, including Priestholm (Puffin Island) and The Skerries. The English name Anglesey is Norse, meaning 'Island in the Sea (or Strait)'.

The Norman invasion led to the building of motte type castles at Aberlleiniog on Anglesey and at Caernarfon. Within a few years the half Viking Welsh ruler Gruffudd ap Cynan drove the Norman earls out of north Wales and there followed a long period of peace and prosperity. Monasteries and stone churches were built, and Llywelyn ap Iorwerth (the Great) constructed several castles including Criccieth. On Anglesey, archaeological excavations have revealed the foundations of his court near Newborough, passed on Walk 14. His grandson Llywelyn ap Gruffudd (Llywelyn the Last) was acknowledged Prince of Wales by Henry III, but when Edward I became king more conflict arose culminating in war and Llywelyn was killed in mid Wales. This was the end of Welsh independence and it was the English king's eldest son who was given the title Prince of Wales. A year after his victory, Edward I held a tournament at Nefyn on Lleyn and this was followed by a programme of castle building. During Owain Glyndwr's revolt in 1404 the king's garrison at Criccieth surrendered and the castle was destroyed.

It was the grandchild of an Anglesey man who claimed the English throne in 1485 after defeating Richard III at the Battle of Bosworth. His grandfather was Owain Tudur who was born at Plas Penmynydd off the B5420 on Anglesey. As a young man, Owain went to London to join the court of Henry V. When the king died, his widow Catherine de Valois fell in love with Owain and they secretly married. Their grandson Henry VII founded the Tudor dynasty.

During the Industrial Revolution the tiny fishing village of Amlwch on Anglesey became a boom town when over 1000 people worked the copper mine on Parys Mountain. It was the world's largest copper mine and forty vessels could anchor in the harbour. Shipbuilding developed as an industry. Herring fishing was important on Lleyn and ships were built on the peninsula's beaches.

In the early 19th century, Porth Dinllaen and Holyhead were rivals for the official Irish ferry port. Porth Dinllaen is a safe anchorage and the building of William Madock's embankment across the River Glaslyn at Porthmadog solved one of the major communication problems between north and mid Wales. Tremadog was to be on the route to the port at Porth Dinllaen and inns were built along the proposed route. Meanwhile, Thomas Telford built his new coach road, the present-day A5, and suspension bridge across the Menai Strait. He also built the Stanley Embankment (named after Lord Stanley of Alderley) linking Holy Island to Anglesey. Packet boats had been crossing to Ireland from Holyhead since the 17th century, and when the official decision was taken Porth Dinllaen lost by one vote.

The Chester to Holyhead railway line opened in 1850 after the building of Robert Stephenson's Britannia Bridge across the Menai Strait. A few years later the Cambrian Coast line was extended to Pwllheli, so opening up the Lleyn coast to holiday visitors. Today both Lleyn and Anglesey continue to attract tourists; many become forever captivated by the extraordinary beauty and heritage of these two lovely areas of north Wales.

The Tea Shops

An easy or moderate walk through beautiful scenery combined with a light appetising meal in a cosy tearoom or sheltered tea garden is one of the best formulas for an enjoyable day out in Wales.

Cream teas and a variety of home-made cakes are on offer at most teashops. Some provide Welsh specialities such as bara brith, a yeast fruit bread, and Welsh cakes, griddle cakes made with dried fruit.

Whether a beach café, town tea room or small gift shop, all the tea rooms welcome walkers, but please be considerate and remove wet waterproofs and muddy boots. The chosen establishments are varied and some are in very old buildings, including former fishermen's and pilots' cottages. Some are attached to heritage centres where you can obtain information about the local area.

Although most of the tea shops close for the winter, a few are open all year. It is advisable to check opening hours if walking early or late in the season.

The Walks

All the walks in this guide are circular. In length, they range from 3 to 8½ miles. Most are suitable for families but children must be closely supervised on cliff paths and headlands.

The walks are gentle or only moderately demanding. Almost all follow stretches of coastline, along cliff paths, beaches or lanes, climbing up headlands or to the top of low hills for spectacular views. Walking boots are not essential, but they are recommended for the rougher walks e.g. Holyhead Mountain. Avoid cliff paths in windy weather. You may like to carry light snacks and drinks for a picnic on the longer walks.

The directions and maps in this guidebook should be all you need to complete the walks. The relevant ordnance Survey maps will help you identify features and places that are not mentioned in the text. The most useful maps are the Explorer Series (1:25000). Lleyn Peninsula West (Map number 12) and Lleyn Peninsula East (Map number 13) cover Walks 1-12. Anglesey West (Map number 262) and Anglesey East (Map number 263) cover Walks 13-25.

Public Transport

Almost all the walks are accessible by public transport. Details are given for each walk. Free timetables are available from tourist information centres. Lleyn bus and train information is in the Gwynedd timetables whilst Anglesey has a separate leaflet.

Welsh Place Names

Welsh is spoken as a first language by many people living on Lleyn and Anglesey. Although everyone understands English, place names maybe a bit of a challenge. Learning these pronunciations will help.

A	=	ah
C	=	k (hard)
Dd	=	'th' as in 'the'
E	=	eh
F	=	v
G	=	as in 'go'
I	=	ee
Ll	=	say 'l', hold tongue in this position and blow gently
O	=	oh
Th	=	as in 'through'
W	=	usually as in oo ('cwm' sounds like 'coom')
Y	=	as e in 'the'

A few translations will aid understanding of place names. The following words are used frequently:

Aber	=	estuary, river mouth
Afon	=	river
Allt	=	slope
Arwydd	=	signal
Bach/fach	=	small
Bedd	=	grave
Brith	=	speckled
Bryn	=	hill
Bwa	=	arch
Bwlch	=	pass
Bychan	=	small
Cae	=	field
Caer	=	fort
Capel	=	chapel
Carn	=	cairn
Carreg	=	rock
Castell	=	castle
Cefn	=	ridge
Celli/gelli	=	grove
Coch	=	red
Coed	=	wood
Cors/gors	=	bog, marsh
Craig	=	crag
Croes	=	cross
Cromlech	=	burial chamber
Cwm	=	valley
Dinas	=	fort
Dol/ddol	=	meadow
Du/ddu	=	black
Dwr	=	water
Dyffryn	=	valley
Eglwys	=	church
Ffordd	=	road
Ffridd	=	high pasture
Fynnon	=	well, spring
Glan	=	riverbank
Glas	=	blue, green
Gwyn	=	white
Gwynt	=	wind
Hafod	=	summer dwelling
Hen	=	old
Hendre	=	winter dwelling

Heol	=	road
Isaf	=	below
Llan	=	church
Llyn	=	lake
Llys	=	court, palace
Maen	=	stone
Maes	=	field
Mawr/fawr	=	big
Melin/felin	=	mill
Moel/foel	=	hill
Morfa	=	marsh
Mynachdy	=	monastery
Mynydd	=	mountain
Nant	=	stream
Newydd	=	new
Ogof	=	cave
Pant	=	hollow
Pen	=	head, top
Penrhyn	=	promontory, headland
Pentir	=	headland
Pentre	=	village
Plas	=	mansion
Pont/bont	=	bridge
Porth	=	port
Pwll	=	pool
Rhiw	=	hill
Rhos	=	moorland
Rhyd	=	ford
Sarn	=	causeway
Traeth	=	beach
Tref	=	town
Trwyn	=	promontory
Twr	=	tower
Ty	=	house
Tyddyn	=	small farm
Uchaf	=	upper
Yn	=	in
Ynys	=	island

1. Criccieth

Route: A lovely varied walk which follows the coast for a short distance before turning inland and rising to a fine viewpoint.

Distance: 5 miles.

How to get there: Criccieth is on the A497 west of Porthmadog.

Public Transport: Trains on the Cambrian Coast Line Machynlleth-Pwllheli stop at Criccieth. Buses from Porthmadog, Caernarfon and Pwllheli.

Start: Car park on the eastern esplanade at Criccieth.

Map: Explorer 13.

Criccieth became a resort in Victorian times with the arrival of the Cambrian Coast railway and it is still a tranquil, unspoilt old-fashioned seaside town. The imposing castle on the dramatic headland was established by Llywelyn the Great (Llywelyn ap Iorwerth) about 1230. His castle consisted of the inner ward, to which his grandson Llywelyn the Last added extra defences. After Llywelyn's death near Builth Wells in 1282 the Welsh castles were captured by the English. Criccieth Castle was expanded and improved. Edward I gave Criccieth a charter in 1284, making it a free English borough. Sir William Leyburn was appointed constable on £100 a year with which he had to maintain a garrison. Ten years later a Welsh uprising under Madog ap Llywelyn besieged the castle which held out under Leyburn and his garrison of twenty-nine men, who received supplies by sea.

During this siege, which lasted all winter, forty-one townspeople took refuge in the castle. About 1359 Edward III appointed the first Welsh constable, Sir Howell of the Battle-Axe. A local man, he had fought in the battles of Crechy and Poiters and, returning in honour, he remained constable until he died in 1381. Unrest in Wales during the last years of the 14th century gave rise to the revolt led by Owain Glyndwr. Criccieth Castle was destroyed by the rebels in 1404 and never rebuilt. It is now maintained by Cadw.

Criccieth Castle

The Tea Shop

Caffi Cwrt is in a three-hundred-year-old building, once used for civic meetings. A good selection of sandwiches, scones and home-made cakes, including bara brith and Welsh cakes, are offered. There is a tea garden. Open from Easter to the end of October 10am-5pm, seven days a week.

The Walk

1. Walk along the sea front in the direction of the castle. Pass the lifeboat station and follow the road uphill past the castle. Continue beside the sea. When the road bends right, go ahead on a surfaced path.

2. Go through a kissing gate and follow an enclosed path above the cliffs. Join a wider path and continue ahead, ignoring a right-hand fork. When you reach a house called Cefn Castell take a path to the right of it. At the end of the garden turn left on a

path heading towards the sea. The path bends right above cliffs and descends gradually to the National Trust land of Ynysgain.

3. Continue in the same direction along the beach for about 80 metres. Look for a path that runs above the beach and, at a fence corner, turn right to join a track. Keep a fence on your right and go through gates to follow the track away from the sea. Go under the railway line (or use the stiles to cross it) and continue ahead through a kissing gate onto an enclosed track. Pass the house called Ynysgain Bach and join a track coming from the left. Continue ahead to the A497 and cross the road with care.

4. Turn right on the pavement and follow it until you meet the drive to the Bron Eifion Hotel. Walk along the drive for about 100 metres and then turn left on a track for Bron Eifion Farm. Pass the entrance to a nursery and at a track junction turn left. Cross an old cattle grid and stay on the main track, passing buildings on the left. At a fork bear right, and at a four-way junction ignore other tracks on the left and right to follow the main track to a lane.

5. Turn right along this very pleasant lane. Ignore another lane on the right and, after passing a nursing home on the right and houses on the left, you will reach the B4411.

6. Cross the road and turn left. Almost immediately, turn right to go through a gate onto a track. Pass houses on the left and where the track bends right to a house go ahead through a gate. Follow the green track between old walls and when the left wall ends keep ahead to a kissing gate. Bear right uphill to a fence and follow this on your right to a kissing gate and enclosed path. At the end of the path, emerge on an access track.

7. Turn right and in about 80 metres bear left through a kissing gate onto an enclosed footpath. Follow it to a field. Walk uphill with a wall on your left. Go through a wall gap and keep ahead a few paces before bearing right uphill to the summit of Moel Ednyfed.

The summit of Moel Ednyfed commands extensive panoramic views over Cardigan Bay, Lleyn and towards Snowdonia. In clear conditions Pembrokeshire is visible. To the north stand the isolated peaks of the Lleyn including Yr Eifl and the highest inland peak, Carn Fadryn. Looking

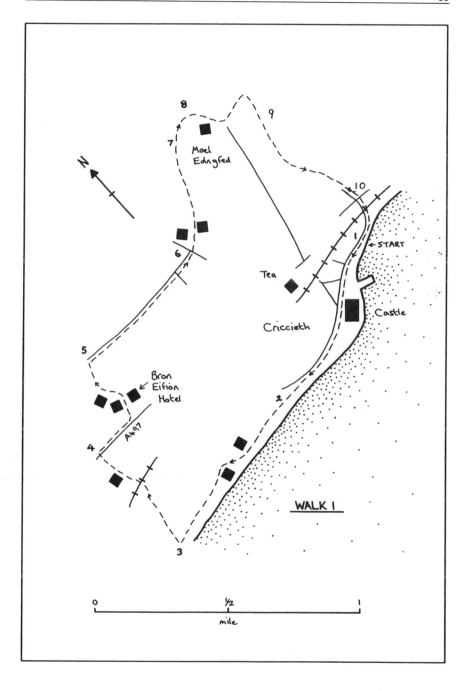

east to Snowdonia, you may be able to pick out the Rhinog range, Moelwyns, Y Cnicht and Snowdon itself.

8. Cross the summit, descending slightly left to a kissing gate. Continue in the same direction to a track and car park at the golf club. Bear right downhill and when you reach a field on the left, cross a stile. (Alternatively, follow the lane to Criccieth). After crossing the stile pass a pool and go through a small quarry. At a junction bear right downhill and soon slant left across a wet area to the left-hand corner of a fence where there is a stile.

9. Cross the stile and, in a few paces, veer slightly right to keep ahead on easier ground. Cross a stream and continue on a better path with the stream nearby on your left. Winding through gorse and reeds, the path leads to a gate and field. Follow the left-hand boundary to a stile above boulders just to the right of a left-hand corner. Continue along the left side of the next field and cross a stream to reach a ladder stile. Maintain your direction to the last ladder stile, which is near a gate.

10. Walk ahead along Geraint Road to the A497. Cross and follow the road ahead over a level crossing to the car park and sea front in Criccieth. For Caffi Cwrt, turn right along the sea front and take the second road on the right uphill. Go over the level crossing. The tea room is on the far left of Y Maes (The Green).

2. Llanystumdwy

Route: A delightful walk along the wooded banks of the Dwyfor River is followed by quiet lanes and fields. The longer walk visits the beach and Dwyfor Estuary.

Distance: 3¼ or 6 miles.

How to get there: Llanystumdwy is off the A497, west of Criccieth.

Public Transport: Buses from Porthmadog, Criccieth and Pwllheli.

Start: Car park in Llanystumdwy.

Map: Explorer 13.

The village of Llanystumdwy is famous for its association with the former statesman and Prime Minister David Lloyd George. David, born in Manchester in 1863, was the son of a schoolmaster William George from Pembrokeshire. Soon after David was born, his father died and his mother (nee Elizabeth Lloyd) moved with David and his sister Mary Ellen to live with her brother Richard at Highgate, opposite the Feathers Inn in Llanystumdwy. Richard Lloyd, a shoemaker and Baptist minister, had a profound influence on young David, whose only formal education was the village school. When David was sixteen he became an articled clerk with a firm of solicitors in Porthmadog, and after passing his exams he set up his own practice. He was keenly interested in politics and in 1890 he won the seat for Caernarfon after the sudden death of the Conservative MP. He rose to become Prime Minister during the years 1916-1922. His boyhood home, Highgate, has been refurbished to show how it would have been in the 1860s.

The Tea Shop

The Dwyfor Café is in a beautiful location with a spacious tea garden on the bank of the Dwyfor River. Lunches, hot snacks, sandwiches and a variety of home-made cakes are on offer. Open Easter-October every day 11am-7pm (sometimes later). Tel: 01766 522719.

The Walk

1. From the car park turn right and walk through the village, passing Lloyd George's home and museum on the right. Just before the bridge over the River Dwyfor turn right on a lane. Shortly beyond the end of the cottages you will see Lloyd George's memorial on the left and a path that descends to the river.

It was Lloyd George's wish that he should be buried on the banks of the River Dwyfor and his grave is marked by a boulder on which he used to sit. Sir Clough Williams Ellis, of Portmeirion fame, de-

Woodland path beside the River Dwyfor

signed the memorial. The walk beside the river is a delight at any time of year. In spring, the woods are carpeted with daffodils, primroses and bluebells. Woodpeckers, flycatcher, treecreeper, nuthatch and warblers may be spotted. Look out for dippers in the river.

2. With the tumbling River Dwyfor on your left, follow a clear path through the woodland. The path crosses a number of plank bridges over small streams and goes through several kissing gates. In about 1½ miles, when a house is in view ahead, bear right with the path to go through an arch and emerge on an access lane.

3. Turn right on the lane and in 600 metres you will pass bunga-

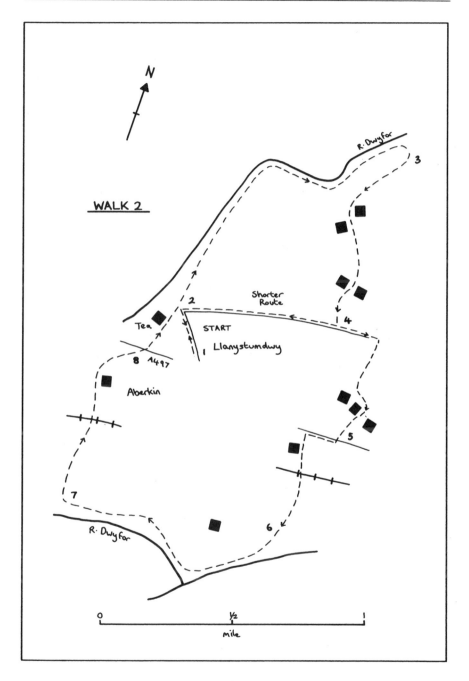

lows on the left. Keep ahead through a gate and immediately bear left to pass farm buildings on your right. Follow the track into a field and continue beside the right boundary to a kissing gate. Walk ahead to a similar gate. Veer right to cross a lawn and pass in front of a house. Bear right and follow the access track to a lane.

4. There is now a choice of walks:

    For the shorter walk turn right along the lane. You will pass the entrance to Ty Newydd, Lloyd George's last home, on your left. In just over half a mile the lane emerges near the bridge over the River Dwyfor. Cross the road to visit the Dwyfor Café or turn left to retrace your steps to the car park.

    For the longer walk turn left on the lane for 300 metres and then bear right through a gate onto the track for Bron Eifion Farm. Follow the track, ignoring tracks off to the left and right. Pass a barn and a house on the right. Cross an old cattle grid and bear right to pass the entrance to a nursery. At the next junction, on the drive coming from Bron Eifion Hotel, bear right to the road.

5. Turn right and in 300 metres turn left on a track for Plas Ynysgain. Where the drive bends right keep ahead over a low stile onto an enclosed track. Pass a house on your right and go under the railway line. Follow the track to the beach and bear right on a path above it.

    The Dwyfor Estuary is a feeding ground for many birds especially herons, curlews, dunlins and redshanks. Look for cormorants on the rocks. In the winter you may see whooper swans, grebes and various species of duck.

6. Continue above or along the beach and when you reach the River Dwyfor follow it inland. Ignore a track on the right and continue ahead over plank bridges. The path bears right to a stile near a gate. Walk ahead beside bushes but shortly bear left to cross more planks. Follow a stone wall on the right for a few metres then go through a gap in the wall. Walk between an old fence on the left and gorse on the right. In about 200 metres go up to a kissing gate and follow a fence on the left to a ladder stile.

7. Turn right beside the wall and fence. At the end of the field there is a stile on the right. Cross the railway line by using the stiles

and continue on a shady track. Cross a stile to the right of a gate and walk ahead to some steps and a stone stile on the left of a gate. Pass Aberkin farmhouse and follow the track to the A497.

8. Cross directly over the road to a small gate. Continue on the path ahead, which emerges near the bridge over the Dwyfor River. The Dwyfor Café is on your left. Bear right to return to the car park.

---

3. Pwllheli

Route: This easy walk climbs to a superb viewpoint above Pwllheli town and harbour. Freshwater springs are passed along the way.

Distance: 3 miles

How to get there: From Caernarfon take the A487 and turn off on the A499. From Porthmadog follow the A497.

Public Transport: Pwllheli is the terminus of the Cambrian Coast railway line. Buses from Caernarfon, Porthmadog and surrounding villages.

Start: The railway station in Pwllheli. Car parks are signposted in the town.

Map: Explorer 12 or 13.

Pwllheli was made a free borough by the Black Prince (Edward III) in 1355. The town became well known for its fishing industry and hundreds of vessels were built in its shipyards during the 18th and 19th Silting up of the harbour needed a government grant of £70,000 in 1903 to dredge it. Nowadays, mainly pleasure craft use this well sheltered haven. It is a good place for bird watching, especially in winter. The arrival of the Cambrian Coast railway in 1867 led to a holiday boom and an expansion in building. Two miles east of the town there is a popular holiday camp. For a long time, Pwllheli has been the shopping and commercial centre of Lleyn and the town is especially busy on a Wednesday, which is market day.

The Tea Shop

The Blue Moon Tea Room is in a narrow blue painted building in Stryd Moch near the centre of Pwllheli. Hot snacks include baked potatoes with various fillings and home-made soup. Almost everything is home-made and there is a delicious selection of cakes. The tea room is open all year Monday to Saturday 9.30am-5pm. From Easter to October, it is also open on Sundays 11am-4pm.

Pwllheli town and harbour from Pen y Garn

The Walk

1. From the railway station cross the road at the traffic lights and turn left. Almost immediately, bear right along Stryd Penllan. When you reach a junction at the end of the road turn right for about 30 metres, then bear left along Kingshead Street. At the next junction, turn right and, in about 200 metres, just before reaching a block of flats, turn left up steps.

2. The path rises and passes behind the flats, bending to the right and then to the left. Follow the walled path to a kissing gate. Do not go through the next kissing gate – there is a spring on the left just before it. Turn left up steps and walk up the field slanting slightly left to have an old broken wall on your right. Go up steps to a footpath signpost and walk straight ahead across the next field to another gate. Follow the left boundary of the field – an old wall with trees growing out of it – to a kissing gate in the left corner.

3. Turn left downhill on a lane. Pass some houses and, after passing a cemetery, turn right on a narrow lane. When it meets a

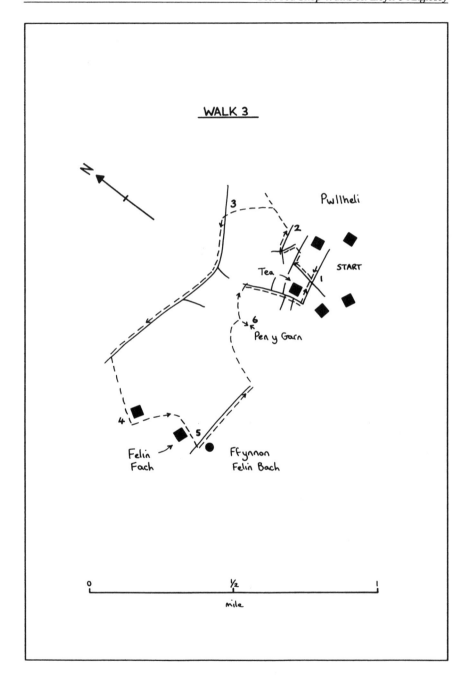

WALK 3

wider lane turn right. Walk uphill and in 600 metres turn left along the access drive to Gwynfryn Farm.

4.   When you reach some buildings continue ahead. Pass Y Bwthyn on the left and go through some gates (there is a squeezable gap to the left of them). In a few metres pass through a long gate and turn left on a track. In about 80 metres, where the track bends left into a field, cross the ladder stile ahead and follow a fence on the left. Go through a gate and continue between hedges to another gate and enclosed track. The track goes downhill and bends to the right, passing through woodland. When you reach buildings at Felin Fach keep to the left and follow the drive to a lane.

5.   On the opposite side of the lane there is a spring (Ffynnon Felin Bach). Turn left on the lane uphill and pass some houses on the right. Shortly before the top of the rise turn left through a kissing gate and follow the clear path ahead. The summit of Pen Y Garn can be seen on your right, At an open area keep ahead on the main path and continue between gorse bushes. Stay on this path until you see a kissing gate on your left. To climb Pen Y Garn turn right on a path uphill. Follow the fence to a corner and then head directly for the summit.

Although Pen Y Garn is less than 250 feet above sea level, its summit commands extensive views of Lleyn, Snowdonia and Cardigan Bay. Below lies Pwllheli harbour and to the west is the headland at Llanbedrog and St Tudwal's Islands.

6.   Leave the summit in the direction of the harbour and when you reach the fence bear left to descend to the kissing gate. Walk ahead across the field to another kissing gate and follow an enclosed path to a road. Turn right downhill and when you reach some cross-roads walk ahead along Stryd Moch. The Blue Moon Tea Room is on your left. Continue along the road to the roundabout and turn left to return to the start at the railway station.

```
┌─────────────────────────────────────────────────────────┐
│                                                         │
│                  4. Llanbedrog                          │
│                                                         │
└─────────────────────────────────────────────────────────┘
```

Route: A steep climb to Mynydd Tir y Cwmwd is rewarded by magnificent views. After circling the headland the route follows inland paths through beautiful countryside.

Distance: 5 miles.

How to get there: Llanbedrog is on the A499, south-west of Pwllheli.

Public Transport: Buses from Pwllheli, Abersoch and Aberdaron.

Start: Car park above Llanbedrog beach.

Map: Explorer 12.

Popular with families, Llanbedrog's sandy beach is well sheltered from westerly winds by the rocky wooded headland of Mynydd Tir y Cwmwd. The village has been settled since the 5th or 6th century when Pedrog, a missionary from Cornwall, arrived here with his followers and established a small church. The present building dates from the 16th century, although the nave may be earlier. During the Civil War the church was used by Cromwell's troops as a stable for their horses and it is believed they destroyed many of the graveyard stones and a stained glass window.

The Tea Shop

Situated above Llanbedrog beach is The Galley bistro and its terrace. The varied menu includes a wide choice of main dishes (including vegetarian) plus delicious baguettes, pastries, cakes and sundaes. The Galley is open from Easter to the end of September, seven days a week, 11am until 6.30pm or later. Evening meals should be booked. Tel: 01758 740730.

The Walk

1. From the car park at Llanbedrog descend the steps to the lane and walk downhill to the beach. Turn right to cross a small bridge and walk along the top of the beach. Pass in front of a long white 17th century cottage (Foxhole) and, at the end of the cot-

Llanbedrog beach and headland

tage, bear right on a path. Before the next house (The Boathouse) veer left on a path and cross some rocks before passing The Boathouse on your right.

2. Bear right to climb a long flight of steps that ascend the wooded headland. Take care not to let young children or dogs dash ahead as you approach the top. The path emerges close to the cliffs near the remains of a statue known as the Tin Man.

    The Tin Man, now much battered by the elements, was built by a local artist, Simon Van du Put, to represent the Celts. From the headland there are fine views in the direction of Pwllheli and, as the walk rounds the headland, towards Abersoch and St Tudwal's Islands. Stonechat, wheatear and yellowhammer may be spotted on the heathland and, sometimes, peregrine, offshore.

3. Pass the statue and take a path bearing right away from the cliff edge. Turn left on another path that winds through heather and over slabs of rock. At a fork take the lower path and bear left at the next fork. There is a maze of paths around the headland. Generally keep bearing left but be careful not to drop very low.

As you round the headland there are fine views of St Tudwal's Islands.

St Tudwal was a 6th century Breton who founded a sanctuary on the eastern island. A priory was established there in the 13th century. Nowadays, seabirds such as razorbill, guillemot, kittiwake and cormorant breed on the island. On the slopes of Mynydd Tir y Cwmwd, granite quarries were worked in the 19th century. The stone was exported to Manchester and further afield. The quarries closed at the beginning of the First World War.

4. At the next junction keep left. The path passes above a quarry and bears right. Ignore a descending path on your left. Shortly before a small ruin take the right-hand path. Pass the garden walls of a house (Mount Pleasant) on your left.

5. Ignore an ascending track on your right – unless you want to visit the summit of the hill. Ignore two drives on your right. Turn right along the next track to pass behind a cottage. After passing a house on your right, where the track ends, take a path which heads towards trees and the chimney of a house. Go through a small gate in a wall and pass a house on your left. Follow the track downhill, ignoring a stile on the right, to emerge on a lane.

6. Turn left on the lane and in a few paces bear right on a track. The track bears right and then left between houses. At the next sharp right bend keep ahead downhill on a path through woodland to reach the A499. Cross the road to a kissing gate and footpath. Pass a well on your right and go through another kissing gate to follow an enclosed footpath. Bear left to pass houses and turn right on a short lane to emerge on the B4413.

7. Cross the road directly to some steps and an enclosed path. Go through a small kissing gate and walk downhill. Bear left on a clear path through a valley, soon following a wall. Cross a stile in the wall and bear left to have the wall on your left. At a path junction, continue on the path nearest the wall. Cross a ladder stile on your left and follow the path to a lane.

8. Turn right on this quiet lane and in 300 metres cross a stile on the right. Walk ahead following the line of an old field boundary on your left. Cross a plank bridge and stiles into the next field

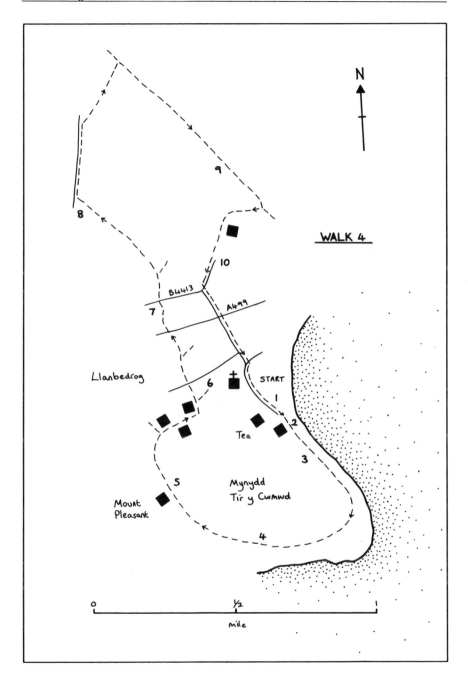

and continue beside a line of trees. Cross a stile and turn right on a track. Go through a gate and continue on the track, which passes beside woodland. After passing through more open land it becomes fenced and reaches a gate and stile.

9. After crossing the stile continue on the track for about 250 metres to a point where there is a cattle grid and track on your left. Now bear right on a path that quickly swings right, descending gradually to the bottom of a valley. Join a fence on the left and in a few metres look for a stile. Cross a bridge over a stream and follow a fence on the left uphill. Go through a kissing gate and walk beside a fence and the walls of a building to reach a stone stile. Continue beside the left-hand wall and fence to a corner stile. Cross and walk ahead to a swing gate next to a field gate and emerge on a lane.

10. Turn left and follow the lane past houses. Ignore a road on the left and walk ahead to the B4413. Turn left downhill and when you meet the A499 cross the road directly to a lane. When this lane bends left turn right to pass St Pedrog's Church and continue on a lane to the car park, 'The Galley' and beach.

5. Abersoch

Route: Tracks and field paths lead to the beautiful secluded beach at Porth Ceiriad. This is a fairly easy walk with few uphill sections.

Distance: 5¼ miles.

How to get there: Abersoch is on the A499, south-west of Pwllheli.

Public Transport: Buses from Pwllheli.

Start: Car park in Lon Gwydryn, signposted off the High Street.

Map: Explorer 12.

Abersoch grew into a small resort in Victorian times and nowadays it is a popular boating and water sports centre. The small harbour and east facing sandy beaches are well sheltered from the prevailing south-westerly winds. St Tudwal's Road, the bay between Llanbedrog headland and Penrhyn Du (Machroes), was considered during the sailing ship era to be one of the safest anchorages in Wales.

Porth Ceiriad

The Tea Shop

Situated in the High Street, Oriel Fach is a popular refreshment stop and has outside tables on the wide pavement. Welsh Rarebit and other toasted snacks are on offer and a selection of home-made cakes. Open February to the end of October, 10.30am-5.30pm. Tel: 01758 713158.

The Walk

1. From the car park in Lon Gwydryn turn left. At the next junction turn right and, after passing the Wylfa Hotel, turn left on the road for the golf course. Pass a car park on the left and continue on a lane.

2. Pass the club house on your right and follow the wide track through the golf course. Continue ahead at a junction of tracks and in another 350 metres emerge on a lane. Walk ahead to Machroes car park and bear right uphill on a track to a junction. Turn left and when there is a private road ahead veer right uphill on a stony track. Pass some spoil heaps and old mine workings on your left.

The Penrhyn Du lead mines are of ancient origin and may have been worked as far back as Roman times. In the 18th and 19th centuries, around 200 men were employed during the busiest periods. Flooding was a serious problem, however, and the workings ceased operating around 1895.

3. Continue to where the track becomes surfaced near a house on the left. Here bear left on a path near a line of boulders and go up steps behind the house. The path leads to a stile and field. Walk beside the right-hand fence to a gate in the top right-hand corner. In the next field bear right to follow an old wall in the direction of Cim Farm. Go through a kissing gate and turn right on a track.

4. At the end of a wall on the left, and at a point where there is another track, cross some grass to a low stile on the left. Slant right through the field and pass behind houses. Follow a fence on the right to a ladder stile. Bear left on a path that passes between old gate posts and cross the middle of the next field to a ladder stile. Now follow the right boundary of a field to a ladder stile and track.

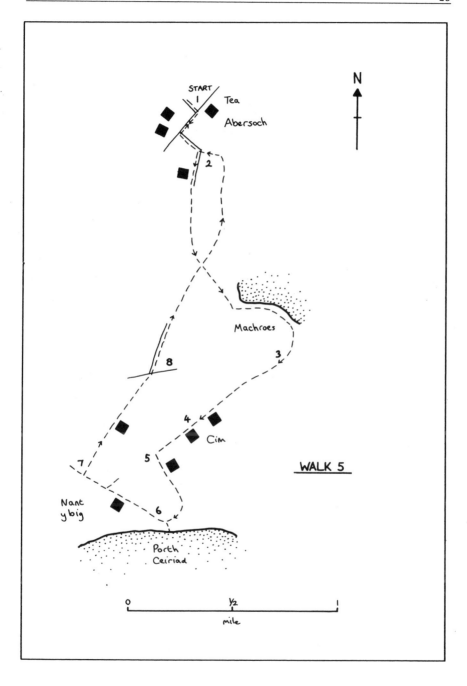

5. Turn left on the access track and ignore a track on the right to a
    car park and caravan site. Walk ahead to cross a stile and follow
    the right-hand fence to a kissing gate. Continue on an enclosed
    path that emerges on a gorse covered hillside. Descend to a kiss-
    ing gate and steps leading to the beach of Porth Ceiriad.

    Adjoining land owned by the National Trust, Porth Ceiriad has a beauti-
    ful sandy beach backed by high cliffs. A large wooden sailing ship, the
    'Franchise' ran aground here in 1855 in thick fog whilst on her way to Liv-
    erpool with a cargo of cotton. No lives were lost but the ship was a total
    wreck and quickly buried by sand. However, the captain was able to save
    2300 bales of cotton, which was carted by road and reshipped to Liver-
    pool from Abersoch.

6. Returning from the beach, go left along the cliff top and follow
    the fence when it goes uphill. Continue beside the fence on a
    clear path that eventually climbs through gorse to a kissing gate
    near the farm of Nant y big. Turn right along the lane and ignore
    the first kissing gate on the right. Continue about another 80
    metres and go through the next kissing gate.

7. Walk ahead with a wall and fence on the left. Cross a ladder stile
    and continue through the next field to a ladder stile in the top
    left corner. Bear right through broad gates and continue ahead to
    pass farm buildings. When you reach the farm house bear right
    to pass in front of it and continue over grass to a hedge. Go
    through a kissing gate and walk downhill on an enclosed path.
    Cross a ladder stile on the right and walk ahead following the
    right-hand boundary of the field. Pass the end of the wall into
    the next field. Now turn left to have an old wall on your left. At
    the end of the field bear right and in about 20 metres go left
    through a kissing gate. Follow the right-hand side of the field to
    another kissing gate. Bear right on a track and emerge on a lane.

8. Turn right and in about 50 metres bear left on a single track road,
    going downhill. Ignore lanes left and right, and continue ahead
    until it emerges at the junction on the golf course. Turn left to re-
    trace your steps into Abersoch or keep ahead to the beach . Bear
    left along the beach until meeting another track near beach huts
    and the car park passed earlier on the walk.

6. Aberdaron

Route: Exhilarating cliff paths lead to Pen y Cil headland and its magnificent views of Bardsey Island. Short sections of the path are narrow and the route should be avoided in windy and/or wet conditions. Fit walkers may like to combine this walk with Walk 7.

Distance: 6 miles.

How to get there: Aberdaron is on the B4413, near the south-west tip of the Lleyn peninsula.

Public Transport: Buses from Pwllheli.

Start: Village car park in Aberdaron.

Map: Explorer 12.

Aberdaron is a small attractive village with steep streets and a sandy beach. The most westerly village on Lleyn, it was important during the Middle Ages as a resting place and embarkation point for pilgrims to Bardsey Island. They probably sheltered in the church before making the hazardous journey across Bardsey Sound. The present church, dedicated to St Hywyn, dates from the 12th century but there has probably been a church on the site from the 6th century. The arched doorway and northern nave are 12th century. Three hundred years later the church was enlarged and a southern nave added. The font is 15th or 16th century. Inside the church there are two 6th century burial stones.

In 1095, Gruffydd ap Cynan was given sanctuary in the church after escaping from the Normans at Chester. The church canons found him a boat to escape to Ireland. Later, Gruffydd ap Rhys, Prince of South Wales, found refuge in the church whilst hiding from Gruffydd ap Cynan and Henry I. The clergy of Aberdaron and Lleyn would not allow the military to go inside the church when they attempted to capture the young prince. During the night he escaped and returned to South Wales.

The most unusual character to be associated with Aberdaron must be Richard Robert Jones, usually known as 'Dic Aberdaron'. A son of a carpenter, he was born in 1780 in a house between Porthoer (Whistling Sands) and Aberdaron. Dic was not interested in becom-

Porth Meudwy, embarkation point for Bardsey Island

ing a carpenter or taking up his father's other trade, fishing. He had no formal education but taught himself to read Welsh and English. From the age of twenty he travelled and became proficient in Hebrew, Latin, Greek, French, German, Italian, Russian and other languages. Some people say he could speak 15 languages whilst others claim it was 35. Quite often he was given books on languages by clergymen or traders in return for manual work. His books were carried in the pockets of his baggy, colourful, patched clothing. He carried a French horn around his neck and his usual companion was a cat. He was known as far away as Liverpool and London, but died in Denbighshire at the age of 63. He was buried in St Asaph.

The Tea Shop

Y Gegin Fawr (The Big Kitchen) was established in AD 1300 as a resting place for pilgrims before they crossed the treacherous sound to Bardsey Island. There is seating outside. The varied menu includes pilgrims' platters, baked potatoes, salads, snacks on toast, sandwiches, cream teas and a selection of home-made cakes. Open from

Easter (or the 1st of April) to the end of October, 7 days a week 10am-5pm. Tel: 01758 760359.

The Walk

1. From the car park turn left and in a few metres turn left again. Ignore a lane on the right and continue uphill for another 400 metres to a footpath signpost opposite a camping site. Turn left to follow a track past bungalows and bear left across a footbridge. Follow a fairly level path along the cliffs and ignore a left-hand path which descends to Porth Simdde at the west end of Aberdaron beach. Looking back there are fine views of Aberdaron, and eastwards across the bay to the islands, Ynys Gwylan-fawr and Ynys Gwylan-fach.

2. In just under one mile the path reaches a kissing gate, and descends through gorse to another gate and steps down to Porth Meudwy. This is the nearest safe embarkation point for Bardsey Island. Cross directly to a footbridge and follow the stepped path to the top of the cliffs. Ignore a stile on the right and continue along the cliff path, which narrows as it passes above Porth Cloch.

3. Go through a small quarry and pass above another inlet, Porth y Pistyll. The path bears right around the bigger inlet of Hen Borth, following a fence. When the fence ends cross a banking, but do not take the clear path ahead. Look for a fainter path on the right going uphill to a National Trust sign. Turn left on a fairly level path along the slopes of Pen y Cil. In about 200 metres you will reach the cliffs and be rewarded with superb views of Bardsey Island.

Pilgrimages to Bardsey Island (Ynys Enlli) started in the Dark Ages. Monks from the monastery at Bangor Iscoed in the Dee valley fled to Bardsey when attacked by the Saxons under King Aethelfrith in AD 616. St Cadfan was the first abbot on Bardsey and he arrived from Brittany about AD 516. Three pilgrimages to Bardsey were considered equal one to Rome. Twenty thousand saints are said to be buried on the island; they include the well known St David and St Beuno. Each monk had a cell made of wattle or stone. The community of cells and church was enclosed by a wall. This was called a llan.

Shortly after AD 1100 the Augustinian canons established an abbey on Bardsey. They also held land on the mainland. In 1533, after the Dissolution of the Monasteries the abbey and its land passed to John Wynn of Bodfel. It is said he was an evil man and supplied pirate ships with food and drink in exchange for goods which he sold on the mainland. Later a fishing and farming community became established on the island. A lighthouse was built in 1821. In the early part of the 20th century there were ninety inhabitants, whose main occupations were collecting the eggs of seabirds, fishing and selling rabbit skins. The landlord, Lord Newborough, appointed an islander with the title of 'king' to collect rent and settle disputes. The last appointed 'king' was Love Pritchard who died in 1926. Bardsey is now under the protection of the Bardsey Island Trust, and is a National Nature Reserve with a field observatory, important for recording birds on passage. Chough, Manx shearwater, kittiwake, guillemot and razorbill nest on the island.

4. Bear right uphill following the cliffs above the large cove Parwyd. From the cairn on top of Pen y Cil there are fine views of Mynydd Mawr at the tip of the peninsula. On the eastern side of Pen y Cil headland there was once a court (Llys y Cil) through which the monastery on Bardsey Island managed its properties on the Lleyn peninsula. Walk away from the cove to cross a ladder stile. Turn left to a field gate.

5. Follow the right boundary of the field and cross a ladder stile onto more National Trust land, Bychestyn. (At this point, you join Walk 7). This is a good place for spotting choughs. Continue beside the right-hand fence in the direction of Mynydd Mawr. Go through a gate onto an enclosed track. When it reaches another track turn right along a lane. Follow it around a right bend (where it leaves Walk 7) and in another 800 metres ignore a lane on the right.

6. In a few more metres turn right along the next lane, passing a farmhouse on the left and buildings on the right. In 200 metres, just before the lane bends right, turn left on a track. Go through gateposts and bear right to go through a gate on your right into a field. Continue over a ladder stile and follow the left boundary of fields until there is a stile on your left. Slant slightly left to join a left-hand fence and hedge. Walk towards the sea, enjoying

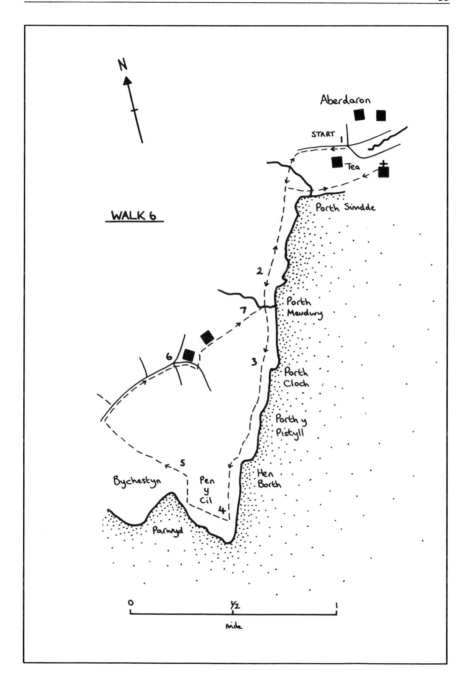

N

Aberdaron

START

Tea

WALK 6

Porth Simdde

2

Porth
Meudwy

7

6

3

Porth
Cloch

Porth y
Pistyll

5

Bychestyn

Pen
y
Cil

Hen
Borth

4

Parwyd

0   ½ |
          Mile

lovely views. Cross the stile seen earlier on the walk to emerge on the cliff path.

7. Turn left to descend steps to Porth Meudwy and retrace your steps to Aberdaron. If the tide is out, instead of following the lane to the start, you could descend the path to Porth Simdde, then cross the stream and walk along the beach to the village.

7. Uwchmynydd

Route: This beautiful walk explores the western extremity of the Lleyn peninsula. Views of the coastline and Bardsey Island are magnificent. Energetic walkers could combine this walk with Walk 6 from Aberdaron.

Distance: 4 miles

How to get there: Continue west from Aberdaron. In 2 miles, after crossing a cattle grid, you will reach the grassy car park below Mynydd Mawr.

Public Transport: Buses to Aberdaron (2 miles from the start) from Pwllheli.

Start: National Trust car park below Mynydd Mawr at Braich y Pwll.

Map: Explorer 12.

The western extremity of the Lleyn peninsula consists of beautiful wild heathland owned by the National Trust. Chough, raven, fulmar, razorbill, kittiwake, guillemot and several species of gull nest on the cliffs. On the headland itself look for wheatear, stonechat and meadow pipit. From the summit of Mynydd Mawr and the south facing cliffs there are spectacular views of Bardsey Island (Ynys Enlli). The island, just under two miles from the mainland, has a large population of Manx shearwaters and from its bird observatory many rare migrant species have been recorded.

The Tea Shop

Ty Mawr Tea Room is in a farmhouse building which is about three hundred years old. Sandwiches, cream teas and a variety of home-made cakes, including banana cake, are on offer. The tea room is open for a week at Easter and every weekend until Spring bank holiday. It is then open every day until mid October. Hours of opening are 11.30am until 6pm. Tel: 01758 760514.

The Walk

1. From the lower car park follow the lane uphill to another parking area on the top of Mynydd Mawr. A small coastal heritage

exhibition is located in the old coastguard lookout. Continue on a concrete path in the direction of Bardsey Island. Descend some steps and shortly bear left on a path that contours the hillside. In about 500 metres, look for the site of St Mary's Chapel, below a hill.

Bardsey Island from Mynydd Mawr

Only the foundations remain of St Mary's Chapel. It appears to have been a large building surrounded by an enclosure. Some authorities claim it was a church while others say it was probably a farmhouse. Ffynnon Fair, St Mary's Well, lies in rocks below the chapel. Although covered by sea water at high tide, the water is said to be always fresh. There are several folk beliefs attached to the well. Wishes were granted to pilgrims who could carry water from the well in the mouth without swallowing, or in the palm without spilling, whilst returning to the chapel and walking around it three times. Traditionally, it was believed pilgrims embarked from here to Bardsey, but although the headland is very close to the island it is unlikely that boats would navigate through the perilous currents of the sound to the small rocky cove near the well.

2.   Join a clear descending path in a valley. To view St Mary's Well (not recommended for young children) bear right to some rock

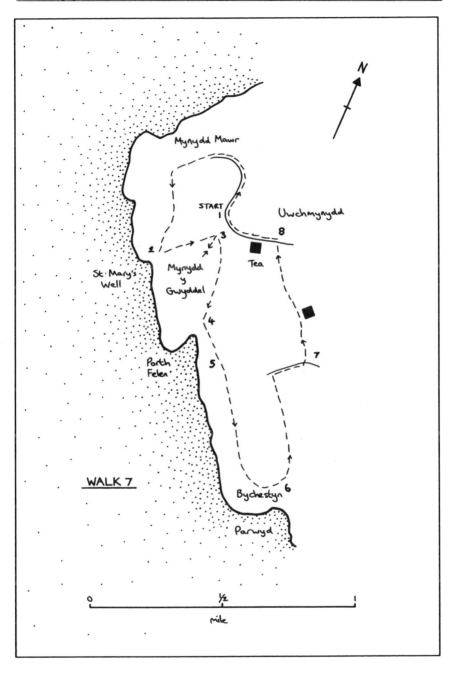

N

Mynydd Mawr

START

Uwchmynydd

8

2

3

Tea

St. Mary's
Well

Mynydd
y
Gwyddel

4

7

Porth
Felen

5

WALK 7

6

Bychestyn

Parwyd

0   ½
mile

steps. Take care here. The scramble to the well is only possible at low tide. To continue the walk, head inland on the path through the valley until you meet a wall.

3. A path on the right rises to the summit of Mynydd y Gwyddel with fine views of the coastline. Return to the wall and bear right on a path to have the wall on your left. In about 50 metres the wall bends right. Continue almost to the cove of Porth Felen and cross a ladder stile.

4. Walk ahead with the sea on your right to a fence corner where there is another ladder stile. Continue ahead, at first through some gorse, and then with a fence on your left. In about 400 metres you will pass, on your left, a gate that leads to a track. Ignore it and stay beside the fence for another 30 metres then slant right to a pair of stiles.

5. Continue over open ground with the sea on your right. In about 500 metres, when opposite the little island called Carreg Ddu, and where there is much steeper ground ahead, bear left inland on a clear path. Keep to the right and shortly reach the vertical cliffs of Parlwyd.

6. When you reach a fence turn left and in another 100 metres you will arrive at a corner stile and a National Trust sign (Bychestyn). Turn left to have a fence on your right. (At this point the route joins Walk 6). Follow the path through a gate onto an enclosed track. When it meets another track, coming from the left, turn right along a lane. In 200 metres, where the lane bends right, turn left on a track (leaving Walk 6).

7. At the end of the track go through the gate ahead. Follow the right boundary of the field to a ladder stile. Bear half right to another stile in the corner of the field. Turn left to a gate where there is a stile to the right of it. Walk ahead on a clear track with a fence on the left. Ignore a track coming from a house on the left, and keep ahead, with a fence now on the right. Go through a gate onto a lane.

8. Turn left and in a few metres you will see Ty Mawr Tea Room on your left. Continue along the lane and pass through the gate at the cattle grid onto the National Trust land at Braich y Pwll. Keep ahead to the car park and start of the walk.

8. Whistling Sands

Route: This superb walk follows a remote stretch of coast through National Trust land on the north-west side of the peninsula. You have the option of climbing Mynydd Anelog, a fine viewpoint.

Distance: 6½ miles.

How to get there: Leave the B4413 half a mile west of where it joins the B4412. Follow a minor road south-west for 3 miles to the road leading to Whistling Sands (Porth Oer).

Public Transport: Take a bus from Pwllheli to Aberdaron. From the village Whistling Sands is 2¼ miles north. Alternatively, from Aberdaron follow the lane west for 1¼ miles and join the route at Uwchmynydd Chapel (Direction 6).

Start: Car park above Whistling Sands.

Map: Explorer 12.

The name 'Whistling Sands' comes from the squeak or whistle emitted by the sands when walked on in warm weather. This curious sound, caused by the peculiar shape of the sand particles, can be heard by stamping or sliding the foot on dry firm sand. On the walk, keep a look out for grey seals and choughs.

The Tea Shop

Whistling Sands Beach Café is located directly above the beach. Soup, jacket potatoes, hot pasties and pies, sandwiches and a variety of home-made cakes are on the menu. Ice cream, sweets, chocolate, gifts and beach toys are also on sale. Open from late May until the end of September. The café opens between 10am and 11am and closes between 4pm and 7pm according to the weather. Tel: 01758 760321.

The Walk

1. From the car park walk out to the lane and go downhill to the beach. Bear left across the sand and scramble up some rocks to a

Coast path near Whistling Sands

path. Cross a footbridge and shortly go up steps to follow a zig-zag path to a gate. Continue on a clear path above the grassy cliffs and, after passing above the small island called Dinas Bach, go through a gate. Ignore a gate on the left.

2. Continue on the cliff path passing above another small island, Dinas Fawr. At Porth Orion you will reach a fence corner where the path goes inland. Do not follow it very far, but find a suitable spot to drop down to the valley and pick up a path that descends to a footbridge. Cross a ladder stile and walk straight up the steep slope to the corner of a fence. Follow it on your left to an isolated (unfenced) stile. Continue uphill and when you reach a fork higher up take the main path, which bears right.

3. Cross a ladder stile and continue on a clear path with fine views of the coastline. The path descends then rises to meet a track. Follow the wide track uphill and at a fork take the right-hand track, going uphill. Pass a small fenced off area on the left. The track tops a rise and descends, with views of Mynydd Anelog

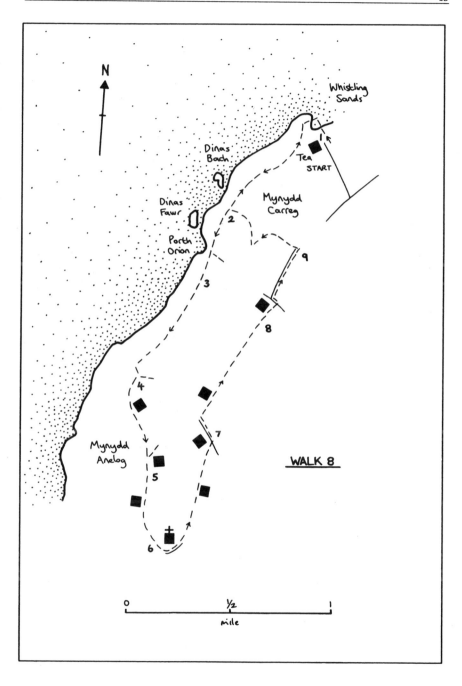

ahead, then heads towards Aberdaron. At a fork turn right towards a house below Mynydd Anelog.

4. Continue beside a wall and when the wall bends left towards the house (Mount Pleasant) take a path slanting left uphill. On joining another path bear left above the house. (Take an ascending path if you wish to reach the summit of Mynydd Anelog). From the path which contours the hill there are fine views to the south-east of Aberdaron and the islands of Ynys Gwylan-fawr and Ynys Gwylan-bach. Bardsey Island is shortly in view. The path descends very gradually and passes behind a cottage.

5. The path drops to a broken wall on the left then immediately leaves it. Keep ahead to another stretch of wall and follow it to a small gate. Pass a field on the right and when a left-hand fence goes uphill stay beside the right-hand fence. On reaching a small cottage on the right bear left on a wide grassy track that goes uphill. It soon descends and follows a fence above a farm. Go through a gate and continue on the track to another gate and access lane. Turn left downhill and, at a junction, bear left.

6. Immediately leave the lane to go uphill passing Uwchmynydd Chapel on your left. Continue on a track, which soon becomes a grassy footpath between bankings. Beyond a gate, walk ahead on a track downhill and look for stone steps and a stile on the left. Cross and follow the right-hand fence of the field, soon passing behind a house. Walk close to the right-hand fence and go through a kissing gate in the right hand corner. Slant to the left to follow a fence and go through a kissing gate on your left. Walk ahead beside a banking on your right. In about 50 metres turn right through old gate posts and walk downhill in the direction of a farmhouse. Go through a kissing gate and turn right through gates to a lane.

7. Turn left for 250 metres then bear right on a track to Gors Farm. Pass farm buildings and a pool on the left and go through the gate ahead. Continue beside a left-hand fence and pass another pool. In an open field, slant slightly right to a ladder stile, which has a footbridge on the other side. After crossing another stile walk ahead through the middle of the field, keeping slightly right to pass an old wall on your left. Cross a stile and keep ahead

to a stile near a gate. The next stile is slightly to the left, in the direction of low houses.

8. Now follow the right-hand boundary of the field to the next stile. Keep ahead to another stile, which is in the fence halfway along the field. Cross a plank bridge and pass a house on the left. Go up steps and cross a stile to emerge on a lane. Turn left then immediately right in the direction of Porth Oer (Whistling Sands). At farm buildings on the left, and at a parking sign, turn left to enter the National Trust property of Carreg

In the 18th and 19th centuries Mynydd Carreg was quarried for jasper, a quartz containing iron and clay. Carreg Plas nearby was once the home of Welsh chieftains.

9. Pass a parking place and go through a kissing gate. Cross, or walk around, the hill and descend towards the coast. Go through a kissing gate onto an enclosed path. When you reach the cliff path turn right and retrace your steps to Whistling Sands, the café and car park.

9. Llangwnnadl

Route: This very lovely walk is quite strenuous with some short steep up and down sections on the coastal path. It may be wet or rough underfoot in places. The last part of the walk is easy, along lanes and field paths.

Distance: 6¾ miles.

How to get there: Leave the B4417 3¼ miles south-west of Tudweiliog for a lane signposted Llangwnnadl and Porth Colmon. Turn right at the cross-roads for Traeth Penllech car park.

Public Transport: From Pwllheli two buses a day (No. 17B) go through Llangwnnadl, passing Siop y Bont. Alternatively, take the No. 17 Pwllheli Aberdaron bus and get off at Pen y Groeslon, 700 metres off route (Direction 6).

Start: Traeth Penllech car park.

Map: Explorer 12.

The Tea Shop

Siop y Bont is a general stores with a small tea garden near the river. Home-made scones, pasties and pies are on offer. Also tea, coffee, hot chocolate and cold drinks. Usually open all year, 7 days a week (closed Christmas Day and New Year's Day). Shop hours 8am-8pm. Food is served 9.30am-5.30pm. Tel: 01758 770240.

The Walk

1. From the car park bear left to cross the bridge and almost immediately turn left on a path. Go through a small gate and keep ahead above a stream to another gate. The path eventually bears right and descends to the beach.

   Although Traeth Penllech is one of the longest sandy beaches on the Lleyn peninsula, being remote, it is rarely crowded.

2. Turn left along the beach and, after crossing the stream, climb the steps to view the waterfalls. Continue along the cliff path. If the tide is out you may prefer to walk along the beach to a point

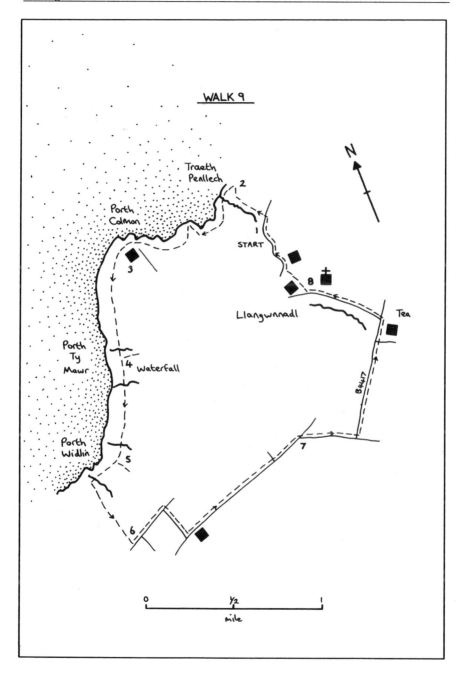

WALK 9

Traeth
Penllech

Porth
Colmon

START

2

3

8

Llangwnnadl

Tea

Porth
Ty
Mawr

4 Waterfall

B4417

Porth
Widlin

5

7

6

N

0   ½   1
mile

where the cliff path descends to a broad gate. Go through the gate then bear right uphill to a seat near a fence. Follow the fence along the top of the cliffs and cross a stile. Continue beside a banking and shortly cross over to a field, following its edge to a kissing gate. Descend to the lane end at Porth Colmon.

3. Bear right towards the right side of the cottage and go down to a footbridge and kissing gate. Take the stepped path up to the cliffs and follow a path beside a banking. Cross a stile and continue ahead along the cliffs. This section of the coastal path is rarely walked. In about ¾ mile you will reach a footpath signpost at an inlet. Descend carefully to cross the stream in the valley. A grassy path descends to the cove, Porth Ty Mawr.

In 1901 the *SS Stewart* foundered hereabouts in a gale. As well as carpets, furniture and other household goods, the ship was carrying a large cargo of whisky. It is said that the cases of whisky vanished before the arrival of the customs authorities. They were whisked away by the locals and hidden in wells, haystacks and rabbit warrens to be drunk during the long winter nights. There is a rumour that some hiding places were forgotten and bottles of whisky still lie hidden in rabbit burrows and other secret places.

4. From the stream, climb to a ladder stile and walk directly up the cliff slope. Continue along the cliffs and, further on, cross a footbridge near a waterfall. Go up to the cliffs again and when the path descends to cross a boggy section stay near the fence. In about another 200 metres ignore a stile on the left and cross the ladder stile ahead.

5. Bear right along the cliff top to Porth Widlin. Descend to cross a stream then turn left to follow the stream to where it meets a fence. Bear right to a kissing gate beside a field gate. Walk inland and go through a gate into the next field. Keep ahead to a corner hedge on a banking and follow it on your left to a stile near a gate.

6. Turn left along the lane and ignore the first lane on the right. Take the next lane on your right and when it meets another lane, turn left. Pass farm buildings on the right and a pool on the left. In spring, the hedgerows beside the lane are thick with wayside flowers. Ignore a lane on the left.

7. When you reach a wider lane, turn right. Pass a chapel and at the next junction turn left in the direction of Tudweiliog. The lane

descends to the refreshment stop at Siop y Bont, which is on your right. Continue a few more metres along the road, and then turn left on the road signposted Llangwnnadl and Porth Colmon. In about 600 metres you will reach Llangwnnadl Church.

Llangwnnadl Church was founded in the 6th century when St Gwynhoedl and his family settled here. The original building was made of timber, and in Norman times a stone church was built. It was a halt on the pilgrim's route to Bardsey Island and this popularity made it necessary to enlarge the building by adding a south aisle, arcade and south doorway. In Tudor times, the church was enlarged again by the addition of the north aisle and arcade. Inscriptions on the pillars in the north arcade record the burial of St Gwynhoedl and the building of the aisle. Outside the church, near the door, there is a gravestone to Griffith Griffiths who died in the 18th century having lived under nine sovereigns. The stump of a medieval cross is in the churchyard. It has a sundial on the top.

Stump of medieval cross in Llangwnnadl churchyard

8. Continue along the lane and in about 100 metres turn right at a footpath signpost to pass the old school on your left. Go through a kissing gate and keep ahead, following the left boundary of the field to a stile and footbridge in the left corner. Follow the left hedge of the next field, sometimes between bushes, to stone steps. Continue beside a left-hand fence to a corner, then keep ahead through the open field to a plank bridge and ladder stile near a gate. Turn right along the lane and follow it downhill to the car park and starting place.

---

10. Morfa Nefyn

Route: This is a superb walk with magnificent views. After following a stretch of beach to Porth Dinllaen the route continues on cliffs around the headland. Some of the walk is alongside a golf course.

Distance: 5½ miles.

How to get there: Morfa Nefyn is on the B4412, off the A497. Leave the B4412 at the Linksbury Hotel.

Public Transport: Buses from Pwllheli.

Start: Car park off Lon Golff, above Morfa Nefyn beach.

Map: Explorer 12.

The Tea Shop

The Craft Shop in Edern not only sells delightful Welsh made crafts but also offers home-made shortbread, teas, coffees and soft drinks. Open Easter to October, 7 days a week, 10am-5pm. Tel: 01758 721314.

The Walk

1. From the far end of the car park take the path down to the lane. Follow it to the beach and turn left. Pass in front of the first house and shortly follow a track behind the house on stilts. (If the tide is very high return to the car park and walk out to the lane. Turn right to the golf club and continue through a kissing gate. Follow the track through the golf course to Porth Dinllaen).

   The building on stilts was once a warehouse known as Warws Dora. (Dora's Warehouse). Dora was one of the steamships owned by the Aberdovey and Barmouth Steamship Company which carried cargoes of groceries and other provisions between Liverpool, Porth Dinllaen, Barmouth and Aberdovey. The 300-ton vessel also provided a passenger service for people shopping in Liverpool. David Williams of Morfa Nefyn became captain in 1909 and he remained captain during the First World War when Dora was commandeered to trade between Liverpool

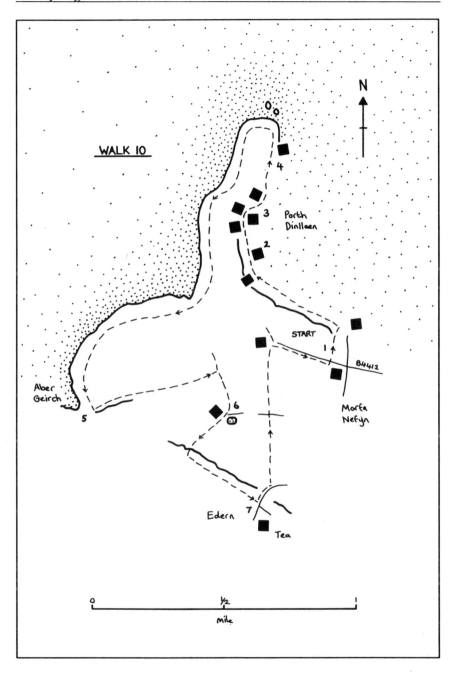

WALK 10

N

0 0

4

Porth
Dinllaen

3

2

START

1

B4412

Aber
Geirch

5

6

7
Edern

Tea

Morfa
Nefyn

0   ½   1
                   mile

and Belfast. On returning from Belfast in May 1917 the steamship was intercepted by a German submarine. After Captain Williams and his crew obeyed orders to abandon ship and take to the lifeboats, Dora was torpedoed.

2. **Cross a small beach to the tiny hamlet of Porth Dinllaen.**

In the 18th and 19th centuries the picturesque hamlet of Porth Dinllaen was a bustling port with a shipyard and hotels catering for travellers. In one year alone (1804) over 650 ships called. The sheltered bay was expected to become the ferry terminal for Ireland but, fortunately, was defeated by one vote in Parliament. Holyhead won. This tranquil stretch of coast is now owned by the National Trust. There are splendid views across the bay to Yr Eifl mountains.

3. **Walk between some houses and follow a path around the coast, over rock and shingle in places, to the lifeboat station.**

Many ships have been wrecked in Caernarfon Bay. The first lifeboat was established here in 1864. Although the lifeboat saved many lives, in the first few years it was not always practical to go out. In 1881 the engines of the *SS Cyprian* failed during a gale in Caernarfon Bay and she lost her anchors. The captain gave up his own life jacket to a young stowaway and a little while later the ship foundered near Aber Geirch. Captain Strachan and 18 of his crew were drowned. The lifeboat was criticised for not going to the Cyprian's aid, but a RNLI inquiry concluded the lifeboat could not have saved them.

4. Turn left along the slip-way and in a few metres bear right on a narrow path. Follow it around the headland. Look out for seals which bask on rocks close to the cliffs. Go up to the old look out tower. On a clear day there are extensive views over Lleyn and to Holyhead Mountain on Anglesey. With the sea below on your right, follow the edge of the golf course. Eventually you will reach a small headland overlooking Aber Geirch. This small bay has a pipeline running out into the sea.

5. Go inland following a path above the bay in the direction of a small hut. Cross a stile to the right of it. Descend to a stream and footbridge, where irises grow. Ignore the footbridge and turn left on a track. Go through a kissing gate in the top left-hand corner of the field and follow the left fence through a large field to a lad-

Porth Dinllaen

der stile. Turn right on a path. Pass a barrier and follow a wall on the left to a track near a pond. (it may be dried up).

6. Slant right to go through a field gate. Bear right and pass behind a farm. Go downhill following the right edge of the field. Cross a stream and turn left to have the stream on your left. Follow a path through gorse to a kissing gate. Continue beside the stream. On reaching a bridge, bear right for 100 metres to the refreshment stop at The Craft Shop in Edern.

7. Retrace your steps and cross the bridge. Follow the road uphill for about 100 metres to a kissing gate on the left. Walk beside the left-hand boundary of the field uphill and descend a little to a kissing gate. Cross a track to a similar gate and continue with a banking and old wall on the left. Keep ahead following the left boundary of fields and emerge between buildings at the golf club. On reaching the lane turn right to the car park.

11. Llithfaen

Route: An interesting but fairly strenuous walk with a steep climb at the end. The longer route visits St Beuno's tiny church at Pistyll.

Distance: 3 or 5½ miles.

How to get there: North of Llanaelhaearn leave the A499 for the B4417. At the cross-roads in Llithfaen turn right (north) to the car park.

Public Transport: Buses from Pwllheli to Llithfaen, ½ mile from the start.

Start: Car park above Nant Gwrtheyrn, north of Llithfaen.

Map: Explorer 12.

The Tea Shop

Near the Welsh Language Centre in Nant Gwrtheyrn you will find Caffi Meinir. There are indoor and outdoor tables. Lunches, teas and a variety of cakes are on offer. Ice cream and cold drinks are also on sale. If you know any Welsh, practise speaking it here! Opening hours are variable, but in summer the café is open every day from lunch time until evening. Tel: 01758 750442.

The Walk

1. From the car park walk back along the lane. Shortly after passing a track on the left, take a path on the right slanting through heather and gorse towards a bridle-way sign. Follow the right-hand boundary of the field and continue beside it when it bears right to a gate. Go through the gate and follow a green track. When the wall bends left go through a gate. Walk ahead across open ground. In about 100 metres you will join a clearer path.

2. Continue ahead with lovely views of Nefyn Bay and Porth Dinllaen. After passing an old field boundary the path descends slightly left to a field gate. Bear right, soon following a wall on the right and go through a small gate in this wall. With the wall now on your left, continue beside it when it bears right. Ignore a

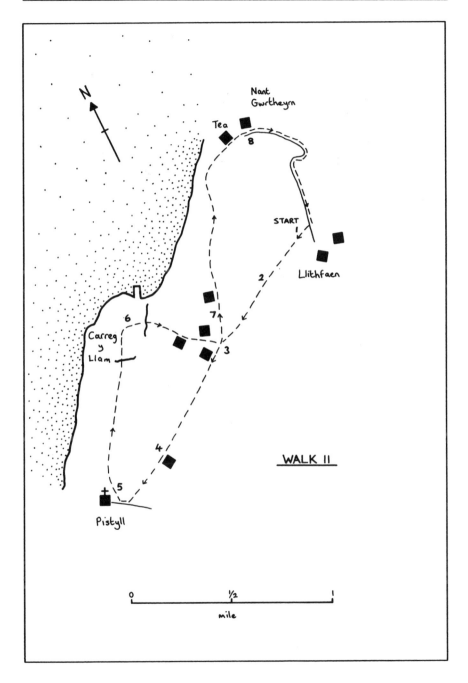

WALK 11

stile and gate on the left. Walk downhill beside the wall. Cross a stile and emerge on a track near a fork. For the shorter walk turn right on the higher track and miss out all the directions until you reach point (Direction) 7.

3. For the longer walk, which goes to Pistyll, turn right on the lower track and, in a few metres, bear left to a ladder stile. Follow the right side of the field to a gate and farm drive. Turn right on the drive but in a few paces go through a gate which is to the left of the first cottage. Cross a lawn to another gate and follow a short enclosed track into a field. Keep ahead with a fence nearby on your right. Cross a stile in the corner and walk ahead, uphill, through a large field, slanting very slightly left. After topping a rise you will see a ladder stile to the right of a line of telegraph poles. Cross it and follow the fence downhill. Cross a stile near farm buildings.

4. Continue ahead past a building and cross a corner stile. Walk downhill on a wide path through gorse and bracken. Follow the left-hand wall and fence to a kissing gate. Continue on a clear path which descends the hillside to a kissing gate and lane. Turn right and shortly right again on a track which passes Pistyll Church.

The tiny church at Pistyll is dedicated to St Beuno, who was descended from the Princes of Powys. Famous for the restoration of his niece's head at Holywell, Beuno also founded a collegiate church at Clynnog Fawr on the Lleyn peninsula. Pistyll was on the pilgrim's route to Bardsey and pilgrims could seek refuge in the hospice, inn or monastery. These buildings were on Cefnydd Hill, which was crossed by the footpath on the way to Pistyll.

Celtic font in Pistyll Church

The monks grew fruit, hops and medicinal herbs, some of which still grow in the churchyard. The western part of the present church is 12th century, whilst the eastern end was built 300 years later. The Celtic font is decorated with a design symbolising endlessness. At the base of the south wall there are steps of an entrance to an earlier building. Until about 150 years ago the roof was thatched and the rope holes can still be seen in the medieval roof timbers. At Easter, Harvest time and Christmas the church is decorated with medicinal herbs and other plants. Rushes are strewn on the floor. In the churchyard, near the top wall, is the grave of actor Rupert Davies, TV's French detective Maigret of the 1960s.

5. Continue along the track and go through a gate. Keep ahead on a green track. At the end of the field do not go through the gate directly ahead, but slant slightly left to another gate. Walk on with a fence on the right. Pass through two more fields, following arrows. When you emerge in a field where there is a bracken covered hill ahead bear right uphill to a gate. Turn left on a clear path with a fence nearby on the left. In about 200 metres cross a stream and go through a gap in the wall. Stay on this main path, ignoring a path off it. Follow a fence and in about 200 metres cross a ladder stile onto Carreg y Llam.

The north-west side of Carreg y Llam provides a nesting site for many thousands of birds, such as guillemots, razorbills and kittiwakes. The site is only visible from the sea and it is dangerous to try to observe the birds from the cliff tops, which are 300 feet above the sea.

6. Turn right downhill to emerge on a quarry track. The quarry has not been worked for about 40 years. Bear right and in 50 metres take a left fork. Cross a stream and ignore the steps on the left that descend to the quarry's derelict jetty. Continue on the path uphill, shortly joining the upper track. Cross a stile and follow the enclosed track past houses to the fork met earlier on the walk. Turn left.

7. Follow the track past a house and bear left to a small gate. Go down steps and bear right to descend the hillside, eventually going through some woodland, a Site of Special Scientific Interest. You may see some feral goats on the hillside or in the valley. Cross a stream. The path descends almost to the beach. Follow a

path above the beach, passing some old quarry winding machinery. At a path junction bear right uphill. At a fork, near a rocky
viewpoint, take the right-hand path. It leads to the café in Nant
Gwrtheyrn.

Nant Gwrtheyrn is enclosed by the steep slopes of Yr Eifl, which rises to
nearly 2000 feet. On the north side is Caernarfon Bay. The valley is traditionally the last refuge of the British high king Vortigern who fled here
in the 5th century. He had sought help from the Saxon mercenaries
Hengist and Horsa to fight the Picts and Irish. As a reward he offered
them land but, dissatisfied, they enlisted the help of other Saxons and
advanced on Vortigern's kingdom. The British felt betrayed and turned
on Vortigern. He fled to north Wales and tried to build a castle at Dinas
Emrys near Beddgelert. Attacked again, he came to this isolated valley,
his last refuge. It is said that local people excavated a grave in the valley
about 300 years ago and found a stone coffin containing the bones of a
tall man. There are other stories attached to the valley. Many centuries
ago monks tried to convert its inhabitants, but the villagers drove them
away. In retaliation, the monks put curses on the village. The first one
said no one who died in the village would ever be buried on consecrated
ground. The second curse was that no villagers would ever marry another and the last monk proclaimed the village would be deserted. The
curses appeared to come true. Villagers died by falling over cliffs or
drowning and so were never buried, fulfilling the first curse. To avoid the
second curse the inhabitants looked for partners outside the village. In
time, though, a couple from the village decided to marry. The custom
was for the girl to hide herself on the wedding morning, but this girl could
not be found. During a thunderstorm a year or so later, lightning struck
an oak tree in the valley and revealed a female skeleton in her bridal
dress. The girl must have become trapped in the hollow tree. The village
prospered and it seemed unlikely that the third curse would come true.
In 1863 the village consisted of twenty-four houses built for the workers
of the granite quarries. Supplies were brought in by ship. However, the
quarries closed in the 1930s and by 1960 all inhabitants had left the village. It became derelict, fulfilling the third curse. In 1978 the village was
restored and it is now a National Language Centre for the teaching of
Welsh.

8.   From the café follow the steep lane around some bends to the car
     park and starting place.

12. Caernarfon

Route: A fairly easy walk along a level lane with lovely views across the Menai Strait. The return is through fields and along a cycleway.

Distance: 5¾ miles.

How to get there: Caernarfon is on the A487, south-west of Bangor.

Public Transport: Buses from Bangor, Llandudno and surrounding towns and villages.

Start: Caernarfon Castle, near the harbour. Car park on the quay.

Maps: Landranger 115;Explorer 263.

Caernarfon was fortified long before Edward I built his castle at the mouth of the River Seiont in the 13ᵗʰ century. The most important of the North Wales Roman forts was Segontium, which is half a mile from Caernarfon town centre. An auxiliary infantry fort built to house 1000 men, it was the centre of administration from AD 77 until the end of the fourth century.

Caernarfon Castle stands on the site of a Norman motte and bailey. Built between 1283 and 1327, at a cost of £19,000, the castle covers three acres and has walls seven to nine feet thick. In 1294 Madoc ap Llywelyn stormed the town walls and incomplete castle. Later, Caernarfon withstood the rebellion of Owain Glyndwr when Conwy and Harlech were taken. Although it is only a shell today, it is a complete one. In 1969 Prince Charles was invested with the title Prince of Wales in the castle courtyard.

The Tea Shop

Y Tebot Fach is a cosy small tea room in Castle Street, not far from the entrance to Caernarfon Castle. The varied menu includes jacket potatoes, home-made soup, salads and toasted sandwiches. Cream teas, bara brith and home-made cakes are also on offer. Open mid February to the end of November 10.30am-4.30pm (5pm in Summer) Monday to Saturday. Tel: 01266 678444.

The Walk

1. Follow the castle walls alongside the harbour and cross the Aber Swing Bridge over Afon Seoint. Bear right along the lane, which shortly curves to the left giving fine views across the Menai Strait.

The Menai Strait and Anglesey

Before Telford and Stephenson built their bridge across the Menai Strait, the only way people on Anglesey could travel to the mainland was by ferry. Sometimes these ferries capsized and people drowned. At low tide sandbanks in the strait are exposed, a danger to boats. One particularly tragic accident occurred in 1785 when a ferry with fifty-five passengers left Caernarfon only one hour before low tide. A strong wind made it impossible for the ferry to maintain a safe passage through the narrow channels and the boat ran aground halfway to Abermenai Point. She could not be relaunched and when she filled with water passengers were forced out onto the sandbanks. Other boats came to the rescue but could not approach close enough to rescue them. All were drowned except one man who, after making a raft from an oar and a piece of ship's mast, survived the icy water to reach shore two hours later.

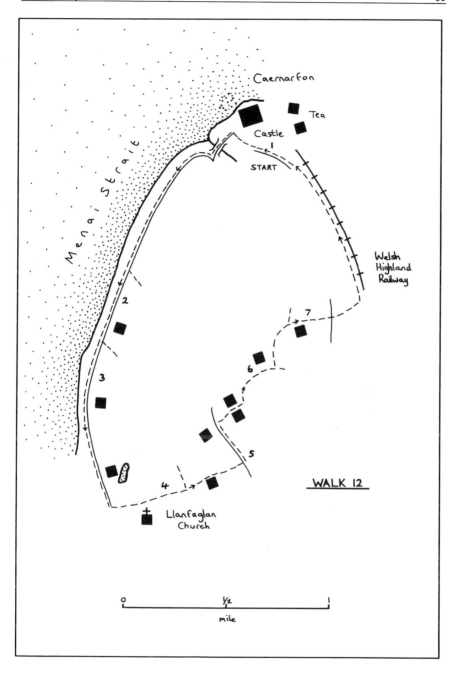

Caernarfon

Tea

Castle

START

1

Menai Straits

Welsh
Highland
Railway

2

3

7

6

5

4

Llanfaglan
Church

WALK 12

0   ½   1
        mile

2. Continue past Caernarfon Golf Course and a small boatyard. Ignore a kissing gate on the left. Ahead is the narrow western entrance to the strait with Abermenai Point on Anglesey and Fort Belan on the opposite side of Foryd Bay.

    During the Napoleonic Wars, at the end of the 18th century, Lord Newborough built Fort Belan at his own expense to guard the Menai Strait against the threat of invasion. The garrison could hold 400 men and had its own drawbridge and dock. In Foryd Bay, especially in autumn and winter, keep a look out for waders such as curlew and redshank.

3. Pass Ty Calch on the left. In another 600 metres you will pass, on the left, another house and then a small pool. In about 50 metres turn left through a kissing gate. Keep ahead on a grassy track and pass Llanfaglan Church on your right.

    Llanfaglan Church is dedicated to St Baglan. Most of the church is 16th century, but 13th century coffin stones form part of the church. Long ago, unknown bodies from wrecks washed up on the shore nearby were buried at this church. In Victorian times, and earlier, it was believed that ghosts of shipwrecked victims took an annual walk to this churchyard.

4. At the churchyard wall corner keep ahead 150 metres to join a track on a bend. Cross a stream and walk ahead to a ladder stile near gates. Follow the right-hand hedge to a kissing gate in a wall. In the next field continue along the right side of the field. Before reaching buildings head uphill to a ladder stile. Continue beside a fence, passing behind the house. Go downhill to a ladder stile and track. Turn left to a junction.

5. Turn left uphill and pass a large chapel on the left. The lane now goes downhill and passes an entrance to a farm on the left. In about another 100 metres turn right through a gate onto a drive. After passing farm buildings the track bears left, passing a house. Continue on a grass track to a field gate. Go uphill in the field, slanting left to a kissing gate near a rock. Bear right and follow the right-hand edge of the field to some trees at a corner. Now walk ahead through the middle of the field to a kissing gate.

6. Bear right through another kissing gate. Follow the access drive of Tyddyn Alys but, just before a left bend, turn left through a gate. Cross the field to another gateway and keep ahead. Go

through a kissing gate next to a gate and bear slightly right into the next field. Walk ahead to another field and when you see a white house ahead follow the left side of the field. Ignore a stone stile on the left. Go through a gate and keep ahead to join the drive coming from the house.

7. Follow the drive downhill to a lane. Turn left and quickly right to pass a plant centre. Walk uphill and pass a house on the left. Go through a gate and turn left on a path beside the Welsh Highland Railway. Follow it to the station in Caernarfon and then keep ahead along pavements to the castle.

13. Newborough Warren

Route: This is a lovely gentle walk through the sand dunes of Newborough Warren, a nature reserve.

Distance: 3½ miles.

How to get there: Leave the A4080 at a bend and small roundabout 1 mile west of Dwyran and ½ mile South of Newborough. Coming from Dwyran, ignore a turning on the left but take the lane ahead for 400 metres to a car park.

Public Transport: Buses from Bangor and Llangefni stop at Penlon (near White Lodge Nursery).

Start: Car park near Llyn Rhos-ddu, off the A480 at Penlon (½ mile south of Newborough).

Maps: Landranger 114; Explorer 263.

A national nature reserve, Newborough Warren is one of the finest dune systems in Britain and the varieties of plants growing here includes wild pansy, lady's bedstraw, meadow saxifrage and various orchids. Lack of cover limits the bird species but there is a possibility of seeing (or hearing) curlew, lapwing, meadow pipit and skylark. Opposite the car park a path leads to a hide overlooking Llyn Rhos-ddu. Great crested grebe, little grebe, ruddy duck and tufted duck are sometimes present.

As early as Elizabethan times marram grass was planted to stabilise the dunes after grassland was lost beneath wind blown sand. Weaving the grass into ropes, baskets, fishermen's nets, brooms and nets became a local industry. Harvesting of the grass took place between August and November. It was left to dry until almost white and was then soaked in water to make it pliable before being woven into plaits. The industry ended in the early 20th century.

The Tea Shop

White Lodge Nursery Tea Shop is a popular stop for walkers visiting Newborough Warren. Pasties, sandwiches, bara brith, scones and a selection of cakes are offered. There is a small sheltered tea garden.

Open from the end of March until the end of September
10.30am-5pm. Tel: 01248 440254.

Newborough Warren

The Walk

1. From the car park turn left to continue in the direction of the
   lane. Follow the wide grassy path for about 600 metres to a kissing gate on the left. It is a few metres before a track on the right.

2. Walk ahead beside the fence to a kissing gate. Continue on a
   path through the dunes following the white posts which are
   placed at intervals to indicate the right of way. In about 1¼ miles
   the path emerges from the dunes and ends on the edge of Traeth
   Abermenai.

   Across the Menai Strait on mainland Wales is the town of Caernarfon
   and its castle with the peaks of Snowdonia behind on the skyline. Ferries
   used to carry passengers to Caernarfon Market from Abermenai Point,
   which is about one mile south-east across the tidal waters of Traeth
   Abermenai. The crossing of the strait can be extremely hazardous and

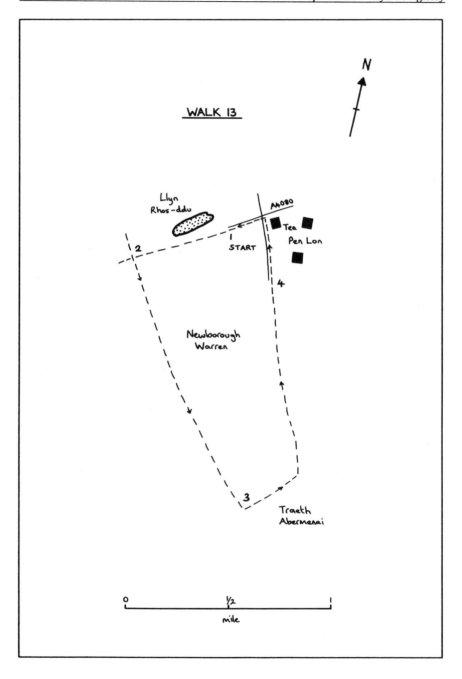

several tragedies occurred (see Walk 12). One of the earliest known disasters was in 1664 when passengers were about to disembark from the ferry at Abermenai Point. The oars had been taken off when an argument broke out between a passenger and the ferryman about an increase in the fare. Nobody noticed the ferry was drifting back into the strait until they were some distance from the shore. Perhaps because of the passengers' panic, the boat capsized and everybody was drowned except for one strong swimmer. Local people believed the tragedy was a form of divine punishment because the wood used to build the boat had been taken from the disused church on Llanddwyn Island (Walk 14). Bird watching can be rewarding here in autumn and winter when waders are usually present.

3. Turn left on a track and in 500 metres look for a white post on the left. Follow the clear path through the dunes and trees until you meet a fence. Keep the fence on your right and before the end of it go through a gate and continue ahead on an enclosed path to a lane.

4. Follow the lane to the roundabout at the bend in the A4080. Turn right for 100 metres to the teashop at White Lodge Nursery or turn left and follow the lane to the start at the car park.

14. Newborough and Llanddwyn Island

Route: A long but superb walk following forest paths, tracks and a remote beach. Llanddwyn Island is sometimes cut off for an hour or two at high tide.

Distance: 8½ miles.

How to get there: Newborough is on the A4080.

Public Transport: Buses from Bangor and Llangefni to Newborough.

Start: Car park near the crossroads in Newborough. It is about 100 metres along the lane signposted 'Traeth Llanddwyn'.

Maps: Landranger 114; Explorer 263.

Newborough was founded In 1303 when the villagers of Llanfaes settled here. They had been forced to move to a New Borough (Niwbwrch) when Edward I built his castle at Beaumaris. They were rehoused on ninety acres of land near the existing village of Rhosyr and the town received a charter. Sea, sand and wind created problems when in the winter of 1330 more than two hundred acres of land and eleven cottages were lost. By Elizabethan times, marram grass was planted on the dunes to stabilise the shifting sands. The making of ropes, mats, baskets and other useful goods from marram grass became a local industry.

The Tea Shop

At the Llys Rhosyr Heritage Centre in the Pritchard Jones Institute there is also a café. Hot snacks, sandwiches, cream teas and cakes are on offer. Open from late May until the end of August on Mondays, Tuesdays, Thursdays and Fridays from 12 noon until 4.30pm.

The Walk

1. From the car park turn right in the direction of the beach. Pass St Peter's Church and, where the lane bends left, look for the remains of a medieval hall on the right.

Lighthouse on Llanddwyn Island

Archaeological excavations at Llys Rhosyr have revealed the foundations of a large medieval hall and another building which may have been the prince's private chamber. The buildings were inside an enclosure thought to be about 65 metres by 80 metres. Some of the uncovered walls are over one metre high. Excavations started in 1992 have recovered artefacts of the 13th and 14th centuries. This was one of several courts on Anglesey which the Welsh princes visited whilst travelling around the island to collect rent from tenants. Law courts and meetings would have been held in the hall. Llywelyn the Great issued a charter in 1237 from Llys Rhosyr.

2. Continue along the lane and ignore another lane on the left. After passing a few houses cross a ladder stile on the right and follow a green track which slants slightly right towards the forest. Cross a stile and follow the path ahead into the trees.

The Forestry Commission took over a large area of the dunes in 1946 and planted mainly Corsican pine, which thrives on sandy soil. There are other coniferous trees here such as Monterey pine, lodgepole pine and Scots pine, also a few deciduous trees including oak, willow and silver birch. Watch out for red squirrels.

3. At a fork in about 100 metres take the right-hand path. When you reach a junction, walk ahead on a track. Maintain this direction, ignoring other tracks. In about 1¼ miles you will reach a small parking area. Bear right on a track which leads to the beach or, after following this track for a few metres, look for a narrow path on the right. It passes through trees and a clearing before emerging on the beach.

4. Bear right along the beach and cross the sand to Llanddwyn Island. From a large information board a good path leads past the ruined church to the pilots' cottages and lighthouse.

On the island you will see some small sheep in an enclosure. They are Soay sheep, an ancient breed similar to those kept by Neolithic and Bronze Age people in Britain. The ruined church was dedicated to St Dwynwen, the patron saint of lovers. She lived in the 5th century and, after an unhappy love affair with a prince called Maelon, she came to this island and became a nun. She built a small church on the site where the 16th century church ruins are now. Below a cleft rock there is a holy well where pilgrims placed a cloth to discover the fortune of their love. If the sacred fish living at the bottom of the well moved the cloth, it was a sign their love was not true. The 25th of January is Saint Dwynwen's Day. The row of cottages was built by Caernarfon harbour trustees in the early years of the 19th century to house the pilots who guided ships into Caernarfon harbour. The white tower below on the left was built as a navigational beacon and some years later, in 1845, the lighthouse was built. It was manned by one of the pilots. In 1972, the shorter tower became an automatic lighthouse. The cannon in front of the cottages was used to alert the lifeboat crew in Newborough. Two of the cottages have been renovated and now house an exhibition and period rooms. They are usually open to the public during the summer months. Look for cormorants drying their wings on the rocks offshore. From the end of the island, there are superb views across Caernarfon Bay to the Lleyn peninsula and Snowdonia.

5. From the lighthouse take a narrow path along the northern side of the island. When you reach the beach, turn left along the shore to have the sea on your left.

One mile north of the island, the wreck of the *Athena* may sometimes be glimpsed at low tide. She was on her way to Liverpool in 1852 when she

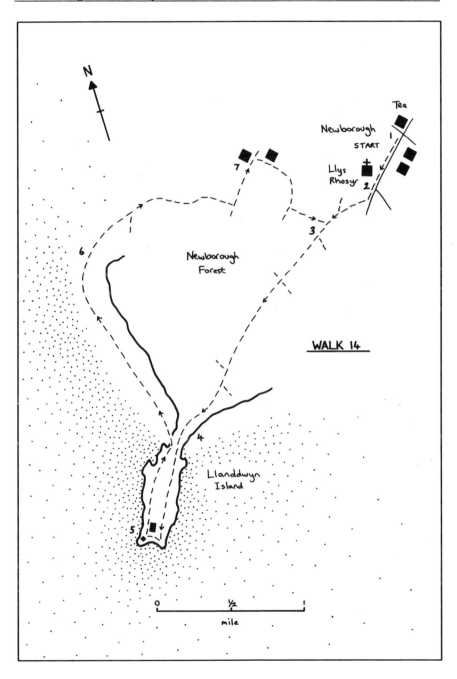

foundered and the Llanddwyn lifeboat crew were called out. High seas prevented the crew from rowing around the island, and a team of horses were brought in to pull the boat over the dunes and sands. The lifeboat was successfully launched nearer the wreck and fourteen men were saved. The vast sands of Malltraeth Estuary are an important feeding ground for wildfowl in winter and during migration. The famous wildfowl artist Charles Tunnicliffe found much inspiration in this area and he lived in Malltraeth for more than thirty years before he died in 1979.

6. In 1¼ miles the dunes bend right into the estuary and Malltraeth Sands. Continue along the beach and just before the end of the dunes bear right on a wide path to join a track running alongside the forest. Turn left. In 500 metres the track bears right then left into the forest. At a junction, turn left and in another 500 metres look for a wooden tower in the trees on the left.

7. Almost opposite the tower, turn right on a track. Pass a small ruin and continue for nearly ¾ mile until you reach a track on the left. Turn left on this track and in 400 metres you will reach the point where you entered the forest. Bear left to retrace your steps to the car park. To visit the heritage centre and café, continue along the road to the A4080. Cross and keep ahead to the institute, which is on your left.

15. Aberffraw

Route: This lovely walk, which has superb views, follows a very attractive stretch of coastline. If the tide is out you may take the opportunity to visit the tiny church of St Cwyran.

Distance: 4¾ miles.

How to get there: Aberffraw is on the A4080, north-west of Newborough. Approaching the village from Newborough, leave the road just before the village, for a minor road on the left.

Public Transport: Buses from Bangor, Llangefni and (infrequently) from Holyhead.

Start: Car park near the old bridge on the east side of the village.

Map: Explorer 262.

Aberffraw is a charming small village built on the west bank of the River Ffraw. The Princes of Gwynedd ruled their kingdom from the royal court here from the 6th century until the death of Llywelyn ap Gruffudd (the Last) in 1282. No trace of their court remains at Aberffraw. The wooden palace was demolished in 1317 and its timbers used in the construction of Edward I's castle at Caernarfon.

The Tea Shop

Llys Llywelyn Tea Room is at the Countryside Heritage Centre, where visitors can see exhibitions about the island's environment. The tea room's menu includes home-made soup, jacket potatoes, salads, scones and cream, bara brith and Welsh cakes. The centre is open from the end of May until September, Tuesday to Saturday 11am-5pm, Sunday lpm-5pm. The tea room stays open in the winter during weekdays but closes at 4pm.

The Walk

1. From the car park cross the humpbacked bridge over Afon Ffraw and walk uphill to the square. Continue ahead and bear left with the road. Pass Stryd Bangor on the left and, where the road turns right, keep ahead on another road, towards the church. Follow

the road around to the left and, after passing a school, turn right on a track. At the end of the houses go through a kissing gate onto a grassy track.

On your left there are lovely views of the river and dunes. The windblown sand dunes on the eastern side of the river have, over the centuries, filled in the large estuary of the River Ffraw, separating Aberffraw from the sea. The village was once a small port with its own shipyard.

2. Go through a kissing gate into a field and keep ahead into another field. Continue in the same direction to an enclosed path, which leads to a track. Pass a house on the right and ignore a track on the left. At a junction turn right and follow the track uphill. Ignore another track on the left. On your right, at the far end of some grass, there is a well. Pass a ruined farmhouse and follow the track around some bends to emerge on a lane.

3. Turn left downhill and follow the lane to the beach at Porth Cwyfan. The walk turns left here, but if you wish to visit the church bear right to the old causeway that leads to the island.

The church of St Cwyfan stands on a tiny island which is isolated at high tide. Founded in the 7th century, it was rebuilt in stone during the 12th

St Cwyfan's Church on its tiny island

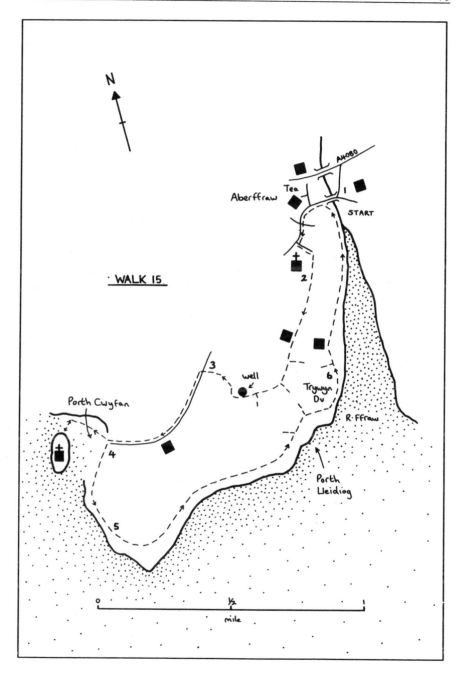

N

Aberffraw

Tea

A4080

START

1

2

WALK 15

3

well

6

Trwyn
Du

Porth Cwyfan

R. Ffraw

4

Porth
Lleidiog

5

0   ½   1
mile

century but has later additions. The wall which surrounds the island was built in the 19th century to counteract erosion. It is thought that St Cwyfan was Irish and a pupil of St Beuno.

4. After visiting the church and retracing your steps, continue along the top of the beach. Cross a sandy section and ascend a short path to a stile on the cliffs. Cross another stile and walk along the cliffs to a headland.

    Seals are frequently seen from this stretch of coast path, which passes above small coves and inlets. They may be seen basking on rocks or in the shallow water below the cliffs. Look out, also, for seabirds such as oystercatchers and cormorants. In spring and summer the cliff tops are clustered with sea pinks, spring squill, stonecrop and other flowers.

5. Follow a wall to a stile and continue beside a fence. Cross a stile and follow the fence as it bears left. Cross two more stiles and shortly leave the fence to bear right above rocks. Follow another fence on the right to a ladder stile. The path eventually descends to a beach at Porth Lleidiog. Walk along the beach and in about 150 metres ignore a path on the left. In another 100 metres go up steps onto another stretch of cliff path. Go through a kissing gate and bear right above a sandy beach. The path bears left but it is worthwhile to follow the coastline around to the next headland.

    The eastern side of the headland of Trwyn Du is on the site of a Bronze Age burial cairn, and some of the stones can be seen protruding through the grass. The cairn was built over a Mesolithic (7000BC) settlement and excavations have uncovered many pieces of flint and chert. Some of these had been made into arrowheads and scrapers. From the headland there are fine views across Caernarfon Bay to the Lleyn peninsula.

6. Return to the main path and follow it to a kissing gate. Keep the river on your right and ignore a track on the left. Pass a house on the left and follow a path to some steps. Walk above a wall and pass a house on the right. When the path joins a track, bear right on a path that descends between a wall and fence. Bear left and follow the track to the bridge and car park. To visit Llys Llywelyn Countryside Centre and Tea Room, do not cross the bridge, but bear left uphill to the square and turn right. In about 60 metres turn left. At the next junction turn right to the centre and tea room.

16. Rhosneigr

Route: This level but varied walk goes around a lake, along quiet field paths and tracks, and returns to the start by following the coast.

Distance: 4¾ miles.

How to get there: About 1½ miles west of Gwalchmai leave the A5 for the A4080 and follow it to Rhosneigr.

Public Transport: Buses from Holyhead and Llangefni.

Start: At the crossroads and clock in Rhosneigr. There is a car park near the library.

Map: Explorer 262.

Built among sand dunes, Rhosneigr has been a popular family resort for about one hundred years. In the 18th century this area was notorious for its shipwrecks and the robbers who plundered them. Vessels were looted while crew and passengers drowned. The gangs even robbed people who reached the shore, instead of assisting them. They were called the Robbers of Crigyll, after the beach on the north side of the village. Lewis Morris, a customs officer and writer who lived in the 18th century, wrote a ballad about three who were sentenced to be hanged at Beaumaris.

The Tea Shop

The Tea Clipper Tea Room was once the sorting office of the old Post Office. There are also tables outside. Soups, sandwiches and a variety of delicious home-made cakes are on offer. The tea room is open almost every day, all year, from 10.30am to 4.30pm. Tel: 01407 810201.

The Walk

1. From the clock walk along Ffordd Maelog and pass the service station on the left. Ignore the first footpath signpost on the left, and continue a few more metres to the next footpath.

2. Turn left through a kissing gate and cross a footbridge. Follow a path beside a fence. When the path emerges in a field, keep ahead beside Llyn Maelog.

    Llyn Maelog was a tidal inlet until windblown sand separated it from the sea. Birds attracted to this reed fringed lake include great crested grebe, little grebe and several species of duck. Reed bunting and sedge warbler are also found here.

Llyn Maelog

3. Follow the shore of the lake. The path is well provided with stiles and kissing gates. At an old quarry, near the head of the lake, keep ahead with gorse on the right. Before reaching a fence, bear right to cross stiles and a footbridge. Continue beside the lake to go through a kissing gate. Cross two more ladder stiles. From the next kissing gate, turn left away from the lake to have bushes and trees on the right.

4. In about 100 metres, just before a derelict house, the path bears right between trees and bushes. Follow the path to a kissing gate and keep ahead along the right side of a field. Go through a kiss-

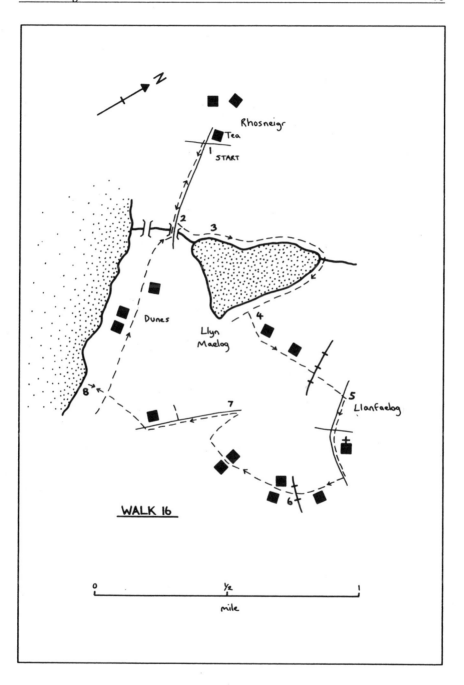

ing gate which is to the left of a field gate. Continue ahead and bear left at the end of the field to a kissing gate in the top left corner of the field. Follow the left boundary of the next field to a stone stile on the left. Turn right on the farm access road. Cross a railway bridge and keep ahead to a road.

5. Turn right for 200 metres to a road junction. Bear right and pass Llanfaelog Post Office. Immediately bear left on another road, and pass a church on the left. In 200 metres turn right along a drive that has the names Awelon and Glan Gors. Pass the house called Awelon on the left. If you look to the left you will see the stump of a windmill. The track bends to the right and crosses a bridge over the railway.

6. The track bends left. In a few metres bear right on a rougher track towards the farm called Glan Gors. Go through a gate and keep ahead to pass the farmhouse on your right. Go through another gate, passing a barn on the left. Cross the field to the corner ahead and ignore a ladder stile on the right. Go over a footbridge and follow the right boundary of a field in the direction of another farm. Cross a ladder stile to the left of a long barn and keep ahead to a track. Turn right to pass the farmhouse on the left and go through the farmyard. Follow the farm access track and emerge on a lane. Turn left to a road.

7. Turn left beside the road and ignore a footpath signpost and ladder stile on the right. Pass Penlon Cottage on the right and, in a few metres, turn right on a track. In about 30 metres, at a bungalow, leave the track to follow a clear path ahead. In about 300 metres you will reach a junction of paths. Keep ahead to the beach.

On the headland half a mile south is Barclodiad y Gawres (The Giantess's Apronful), an important Neolithic burial chamber. It is a passage grave, covered with stones and earth, similar to some found in Ireland. The tomb is remarkable for its stones; some of them are decorated with spirals, zigzags and lozenges. Excavations revealed human bones, and also animal bones from a funerary ritual. The burial chamber is accessible from a footpath which goes around the headland, but the tomb has been partly restored and the interior is barred by a locked gate. The key is obtainable from the Heritage Centre at Aberffraw. Take a torch if you wish to see the patterns closely. There is a car park near the headland.

8. From here you can return to Rhosneigr by walking along the beach (tide permitting) or following a path through the dunes.

To return along the beach: Turn right, with the sea on your left, and in about 700 metres pass some houses. When you reach a river, in another 500 metres, bear right to cross a footbridge. Follow the track to the road and turn left to the start.

To return through the dunes: Return to the path junction and turn left. Pass an old plantation on the right. When you reach a track, keep ahead to pass houses on your left. Before the last building take a path on the right and walk through the dunes. Pass behind Llyn Maelog Hotel and continue ahead for about another 300 metres before bearing right to the road. Turn left into Rhosneigr. At the clock, keep ahead to the tea room, which is on your right.

17. Trearddur Bay

Route: After leaving the inlets at Trearddur Bay, the walk continues along a cliff path through spectacular scenery. On the longer route the path passes close to the cliff edge in places and is not suitable for young children.

Distance: 6 or 7½ miles.

How to get there: Leave the A5 at Valley and take the B4545 to Trearddur Bay.

Public Transport: Buses from Bangor and Holyhead.

Start: Large car park behind the beach at Trearddur Bay.

Map: Explorer 262.

The village of Trearddur stands on a narrow neck of land where Holy Island is less than 400 metres wide. The crescent shaped sandy beach is sheltered by low rocks. Behind the beach, on a sand dune, is the site of a chapel founded by St Ffraid (Bridget). According to legend, she and her maidens fled from Ireland because she did not wish to marry the Irish prince chosen for her by her father. They travelled across the sea on pieces of turf and landed in Trearddur Bay. The turf took root here and on it St Ffraid built her chapel. The chapel was still here in 1780. When it was excavated in 1846 by Stanley it had been buried by sand. In size, it was about 30 feet by 22 feet. There were human bones under the chapel and graves five layers deep. Some may have been from the 5th century. It is thought the graveyard was in use until 300 years ago. Before the promenade was built, storms regularly attacked the churchyard and bones were often found on the beach.

The Tea Shop

The Sea Shanty Café can be found next to the car park behind Trearrddur Bay. Inside, the walls are hung with fishing nets and there are tables outside. All day breakfast, hot snacks, sandwiches, apple pie and a variety of cakes are on offer. Open from April to the

end of September (closed Thursdays) 10am-6pm. Tel: 01407
860788.

The Walk

1. From the car park take one of the paths to the promenade. Turn
   right for a short distance if you wish to see the site of the chapel.
   An information board indicates the site. The walk bears left.
   Have the beach on your right and follow the promenade to a
   road. Bear right and walk uphill. Pass the attractive cove called
   Porth Diana and the smaller Porth Castell. The road bends left
   and passes some houses to reach a fork on open ground.

2. Slant to the right and follow a path through heather scrubland. It
   emerges on a track which enters a caravan site. Cross two tracks
   to another path and continue in the direction of a cove. When
   you reach a track near caravans bear right, and shortly leave the
   track for a path that goes above a caravan. Go left downhill to a
   kissing gate at the lovely cove called Porth-y-garan.

3. Follow a path behind the cove and ignore a path on the left. Continue ahead and pass a pool on the right. After passing a fence
   corner on the left, go around an inlet to have a fence on the right.
   Go through a kissing gate and continue ahead. On reaching a
   wall, follow it inland to the entrance gates of two houses. Cross a
   stile beside the gate of Cefn y Borth and walk beside a wall on
   your left. Go through a wall gap and continue on a path through
   gorse, heather and rocks to kissing gate. Go downhill between
   rocky outcrops and follow the path uphill to a stile. As you approach the stile look right to see a rock arch.

   Black Arch (Bwa Du) was the site of a quarry which supplied marble for
   use in the building of Peterborough, Bristol and Worcester Cathedrals.

4. After crossing the stile go uphill, but in about 60 metres walk
   seawards and look for a small memorial stone.

   The small memorial has an inscription on its seaward side. It reads:
   'Tyger Sep 17th 1819'. It commemorates the intelligence and loyalty of a
   dog who saved his master, a boy and two men. On a voyage from Liverpool their ketch ran into thick fog and hit Maen Piscar, an isolated rock
   about ¾ mile offshore. They were all forced into the water, but only the

dog sensed the direction of the nearest land. It is thought he heard echoes from the cliffs. Trusting the retriever's instinct, the captain followed his direction and helped the two men. The boy held on to Tyger's collar. After taking the boy safely to land, the dog swam back and pulled one of the men by the collar onto the rocks. Tyger then went back to sea twice more to help the other man and his master reach the shore. Completely exhausted, and all his strength gone, Tyger gave his master's hand a lick and died.

The White Arch

5. Follow the cliffs to another rock called White Arch (Bwa Gwyn). It is the site of a china clay quarry. Walk inland about 300 metres to pass behind the rocky cove called Porth Saint. Here you have the option of shortening the walk.

    Shorter walk. Do not cross the footbridge behind Porth Saint. Before reaching it, veer left to cross a small stile. Bear slightly left across the field to a stile in the top left corner. Follow a wide grassy track bounded by old stone walls. Cross a ladder stile and, just before reaching a gate, bear left beside a wall. At a corner continue around the wall to the next corner. Bear right to follow a fence and wall on your left to a kissing gate. Turn left on

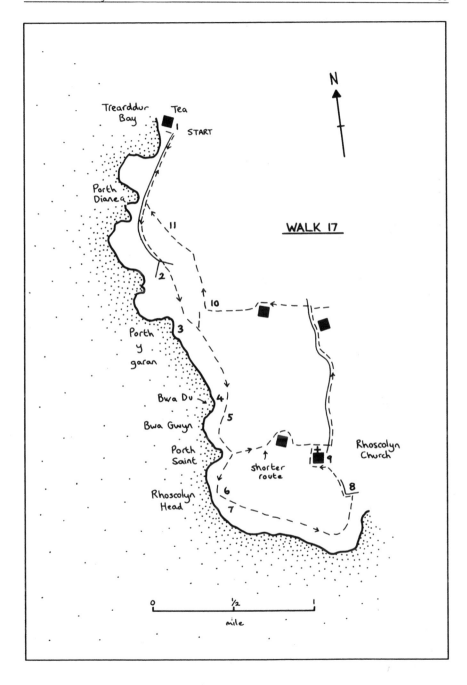

Trearddur Bay

Tea

START

N

Porth Dianea

11

WALK 17

2

10

Porth y garan

3

Bwa Du

4

5

Bwa Gwyn

Porth Saint

Rhoscolyn Church

shorter route

9

Rhoscolyn Head

8

6

7

0   ½   1

mile

the track coming from the farm. Follow it to the churchyard, where you join the longer route (Direction 9).
Longer walk. Cross the footbridge at Porth Saint. Go over a stile and continue with a wall on the left towards Rhoscolyn Head. A short section of the path is railed. The path strays from the wall, but climbs up to meet it again.

Off Rhoscolyn Head in 1855 the Southern Cross sank after hitting a submerged rock in dense fog. The crew of seventeen escaped in the ship's lifeboat, which also hit a rock. The men were able to climb onto a large rock, but had to wait twelve hours for Rhoscolyn's lifeboat to rescue them.

6. Follow the wall around a corner – take care here – to a kissing gate. Walk in the direction of the coastguard lookout and in about 70 metres you will see St Gwenfaen's Well on your right.

    St Gwenfaen's Well is below ground level. Steps descend to the chamber, which has seats in the corners. This holy well was traditionally believed to cure mental illness. It was customary to make an offering of quartz pebbles and these were thrown into the water.

7. Walk up to the lookout – a fine viewpoint. Pass the building on your right and walk ahead, following a grassy path downhill. Go over a slight rise and descend to a kissing gate in a wall. Keep ahead beside a wall, then bear slightly left to cross a stone stile. Cross a track to an enclosed footpath. Follow the path around bends and between bushes to a stile. Cross a field passing between two wells. Go through a kissing gate in the top right corner of the field. Turn left and cross a stile. Walk ahead and shortly before the end of the field bear right to a ladder stile. Follow the left side of the field to another stile and walk towards a house. Pass the garden wall on your left and go through a kissing gate.

8. Turn left on the lane and in a few metres, where the lane bends right, keep ahead through the gate to Ty Weryl. In a few paces take an enclosed path on the right. Go through a small gate and follow the right boundary of the field. Cross a track and go through a kissing gate. Slant slightly right across the field to another kissing gate, which is hidden by a wall. Bear slightly right again towards the corner of a high wall. Continue ahead to a ladder stile. Now bear slightly left to the end of the churchyard and

some hidden steps leading to a path. Follow the churchyard wall on your right and go through a small gate onto a track. Bear right to join the shorter route.

Rhoscolyn Church was founded by St Gwenfaen. Look in the churchyard for the high memorial to the lifeboat men who lost their lives in December 1920 whilst going to the rescue of the steamship Timbo in Caernarfon Bay. Heavy seas and 80mph winds caused the lifeboat crew to turn back and try to find shelter at Llanddwyn. Five of the boatmen, including the coxswain Owen Owens, were swept away during the seven hours it took the boat to reach land. They are buried together in Rhoscolyn churchyard.

9. Pass the church and shortly bear left on a lane. Follow it for 1¼ miles. At a walking man signpost turn left on the access track for Bryn Ffysiwn. Continue past a house. Cross a stile at a gate and in another 150 metres, where the drive goes uphill to a house, take a footpath on the right, keeping roughly ahead. Follow it towards some rocks and bear slightly left to pass rocky outcrops on your right. Shortly beyond the outcrops you will reach a path junction.

10. Turn right uphill on a path through rocks and gorse. In about 70 metres cross a low stone stile. Continue ahead to meet another path and bear right to a stile at a gate. Walk ahead with a caravan site on the left. Do not take any paths leading off to the right or left. Pass a caravan site on the right and emerge at the site's entrance. Bear left and almost immediately turn right into another site. Pass the site's office on the left and turn left to pass the clubhouse on your right. Follow the track as it curves slightly left. Keep a fence on your right and pass bungalows on your left. Continue on grass beside the fence. After passing a cottage on the right, go through a gap in the fence and follow a path to a stone stile. Keep ahead across a lawn to a kissing gate.

11. Cross a drive to another footpath and walk ahead. Bear slightly right around a hillock. When the path forks, go left to a stile and follow a fence on your right. Ignore a stile in it. At the end of the field continue on an enclosed path to a track. Bear right downhill and at a path junction turn left to reach the road at Porth Diana. Bear right to follow your outward route to the start of the walk at Trearddur Bay.

18. South Stack and Holyhead Mountain

Route: A short but strenuous walk with magnificent coastal views. Some of the paths are quite rough and sturdy footwear is essential. Children must be closely supervised on the cliff paths.

Distance: 3 miles.

How to get there: Leave the A5 at Valley and follow the B4545 to Trearddur village. Turn left on a minor road signposted South Stack. Approaching from Holyhead, South Stack is signposted from the outer harbour.

Public Transport: During the summer months there is a bus service from Holyhead to South Stack.

Start: Car park on the left side of the lane approaching South Stack.

Map: Explorer 262.

The Tea Shop

South Stack Kitchen café and restaurant is situated directly above the RSPB visitor centre. The varied menu includes main meals, salads, savoury flans, baked potatoes, toasties and a selection of home baked cakes including bara brith. Open Easter to mid September 10.30am until early evening. Tel: 01407 762181.

The Walk

1. From the back of the car park take the path towards the sea. At a path running directly above the cliffs, turn right to Ellin's Tower.

    Ellin's Tower is a RSPB visitor centre. The building was built in the 19ᵗʰ century by Lord Stanley of Alderley (Liberal MP for Anglesey) as a summerhouse for his wife Ellin. Stanley carried out several archaeological excavations on Holyhead Mountain. After falling into disrepair, the tower was bought by the RSPB in 1980 and it was opened to the public

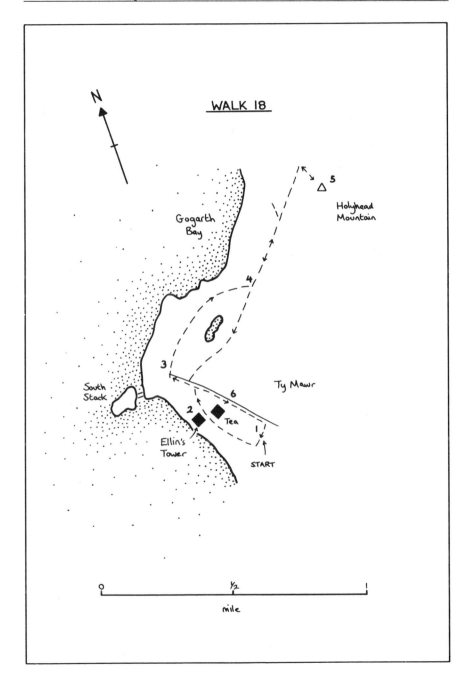

two years later. Below the tower, puffins, guillemots and razorbills nest on the cliffs.

2. From the tower take a path which bears left to the lane. Turn left to steps leading down to South Stack lighthouse.

After being closed for some years, South Stack lighthouse and its suspension bridge have been reopened to the public. (Tickets obtainable at South Stack Kitchen). The first lighthouse was built in 1809 by Daniel Alexander who designed Dartmoor prison. Until South Stack was provided with a suspension bridge in 1827, people visiting the lighthouse were hauled across the chasm in a basket attached to a rope. The lighthouse became automatic in 1984 and its light can be seen twenty-eight miles away. The steps leading down to the lighthouse provide excellent viewpoints of the seabird colonies.

3. At the steps to South Stack lighthouse bear right on a cliff path. Climb to a ruined lookout and continue on the path through heather. As you climb there are fine views of North Stack, Gogarth Bay and Holyhead Mountain. Some 'dishes' come in

Gogarth Bay

view. At a fork in the path on level ground, bear right to a tar-macked track.

4. Cross the track onto a rougher path. Ignore paths on the right and pass the 'dishes' on the left. In another 250 metres bear left at a fork. At the next fork bear right. (The left-hand path de-scends above Gogarth Bay). Continue uphill; the path is stepped in places. When you reach the brow of the hill, turn right on a path to the summit of Holyhead Mountain.

Holyhead Mountain is a superb viewpoint and its panorama covers most of western Anglesey. Views extend to Snowdonia and the Lleyn penin-sula. In very clear conditions it may be possible to see Ireland. Iron Age people built a hill fort (Caer y Twr) on the summit as a refuge from the Irish who carried out frequent raids along the west coast of Britain dur-ing this era. The hill fort covered seventeen acres with a defensive wall on the north and east sides, which still stands to a height of ten feet in places. The entrance passageway is at the north-east corner. No hut circles have been found, but the base of a Roman watchtower can be seen close to the trig. point. From here warnings of approaching boats could be passed to the Roman naval base at Holyhead.

5. Retrace your steps to the tarmacked track near the 'dishes'. Turn left and follow the track to the lane. Bear left and in about 300 metres you will see South Stack Kitchen on the right.

6. Return to the start by following the lane, or from the back of the restaurant take a path to Ellin's Tower and turn left.

Opposite the entrance to the car park a short path leads to an ancient settlement. William Stanley found over fifty huts on the Ty Mawr site when he excavated the settlement in the mid 19th century. Around half that number can be seen today, but those that remain are extremely well preserved. The large round circles were the living quarters, and on their walls wooden posts would have been placed and covered with reeds or straw to form a conical roof. Stanley found slag, crushed quartzite and hearths in the rectangular huts which suggests they were work-shops. Later excavations have provided evidence that the site could have been used intermittently from the Neolithic (New Stone) Age up to the 6th century AD.

19. North Stack

Route: This is a superb walk with spectacular views. A level stroll along the rocky coast is followed by a climb to North Stack. The walk then crosses the side of Holyhead Mountain before descending to the Breakwater Country Park. Steep sections of the walk are short.

Distance: 4 miles.

How to get there: From the sea front in Holyhead follow signs for the Breakwater Country Park.

Public Transport: Trains to Holyhead. Buses from Bangor and towns and villages on Anglesey to Holyhead, 1 mile from the start.

Start: Small car park on the right before the first bridge on the access lane to the Breakwater Country Park.

Map: Explorer 262.

The Tea Shop

Situated in the Breakwater Country Park, the North Wales Wildlife Trust Shop is not exactly a tea shop, but it does offer tea, coffee and biscuits as well as cold drinks and ice cream. Gifts and maps are also on sale. Open at Easter and from the end of May to the end of September every day 1pm-4pm.

The Walk

1. From the car park take the signposted coastal footpath to a small cove. On your right is Holyhead's breakwater.

    The massive structure of Holyhead's breakwater stretches for 1½ miles from Soldier's Point and ends at a lighthouse. It was built as part of a programme by Parliament to construct harbours around Britain where ships could find shelter from storms. Work started in 1845 and 28 years later the breakwater was opened by the Prince of Wales. Limestone quarried on Holyhead Mountain was carried along a tramway to the sea. One of the engineers was John Hawkshaw, who built himself the castellated house at Soldier's Point.

Holyhead's breakwater and nearby coastline

2. Turn left and follow the path through heather and above rocks.
    At a fork take the right-hand path and continue close to the sea.
    The path heads towards a quarry and then bears left in the direc-
    tion of a tall chimney. Emerge on a wide track and turn right.
    You will shortly see a memorial on your right.

    The memorial is to eight missing airmen who were lost in the Irish Sea on
    22 December 1944. The American aircraft should have landed at
    Cheddington but, because of bad weather, was diverted to Atcham, and
    from there to RAF Valley on Anglesey. In poor visibility, the pilot lost ra-
    dio contact while awaiting permission to land, and with the aircraft run-
    ning out of fuel, the crew baled out. It is thought the eight missing
    airmen jumped before being given the order to do so. The pilot and his
    co-pilot parachuted safely to land not far from Holyhead and seconds
    later the pilotless aircraft crashed into the cliffs near North Stack. An
    extensive search was carried out for the missing crew, but they were not
    found. In 1992 divers found the aircraft debris including the propeller
    blade which has been mounted to form the memorial. Another salvaged
    blade has been made into a memorial in North Carolina.

3. Continue ahead through a kissing gate and follow the track up-
    hill. In about 150 metres you will pass the corner of a wall on

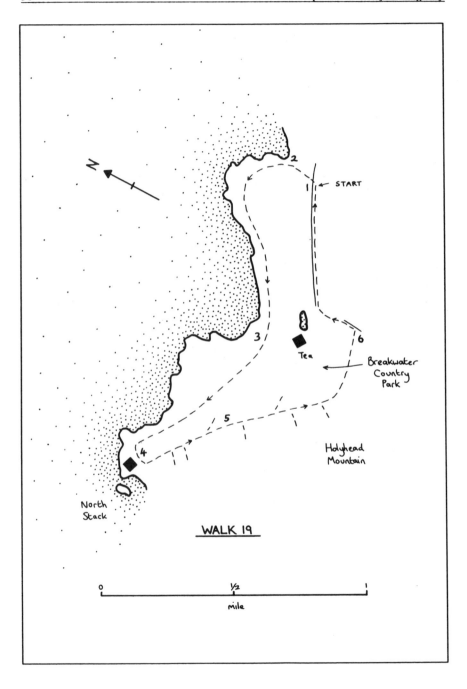

START

2

1

3

Tea

6

Breakwater
Country
Park

5

4

North
Stack

Holyhead
Mountain

WALK 19

0   ½   1
mile

your right. In another 35 metres take a path on the right through the heather. It follows a line of telegraph poles and emerges at buildings near North Stack. Take care if you venture to the end of the headland.

Opposite the headland is the small island called North Stack. Looking left you can see a massive cave and the cliffs of Gogarth Bay, a rock climbing area. Seals may be seen basking on rocks between North and South Stack. In the mid 19th century a fog signal station was constructed on the headland, from where a gun was fired to warn shipping. The footpath to North Stack was used by the donkeys carrying explosives and food from Holyhead to the fog station.

4. Turn left to follow the steep track uphill. In about 350 metres ignore a path going off to the right, and also a clearer path 70 metres later. Stay on the track for another 200 metres, and at a telegraph pole just before the track starts to descend, take a path on the right.

5. With the track below on the left, the path slants gently uphill through heather. It soon becomes clearer and wider with fine views of Holyhead harbour. In 300 metres ignore a path on the right. At a fork in another 400 metres, take the right-hand path. It rises a little and crosses another path. (The path on the right climbs to the summit of Holyhead Mountain). Continue ahead. As you descend, small walled fields are in view below. Ignore a path on the right and bear left. The fields are now on the right. The path passes between walls. At a fork turn left and when you join a drive, keep ahead to a lane.

6. Turn left on the lane. When it ends shortly before the last house on the right, turn left on a path. In about 50 metres it bears right to follow a fence on the left and joins another path. Descend with the fence on your left and with views of the breakwater. Emerge in a disused quarry and turn left to reach a road in the country park. Turn left for refreshments, or turn right and follow the road for 800 metres to the car park.

The Breakwater Country Park was officially opened in 1994. There is a museum, information boards, small pools and picnic areas, as well as the shop. The tall chimney and kilns were built at the beginning of the 20th century for a brickworks.

20. Cemaes

Route: Magnificent views, cliff paths, an unusual church and 19th century industrial remains are the highlights of this superb walk. Short sections of the path are steep or rough and care must be taken near cliff edges.

Distance: 7 miles.

How to get there: Cemaes lies west of Amlwch and north of the A5025.

Public Transport: Buses from Bangor, Amlwch and Holyhead.

Start: Car park signposted off the High Street in Cemaes. There are other car parks on the sea front.

Map: Explorer 262.

Cemaes was the main port on the north coast of Anglesey until Amlwch's growth during the industrial revolution. The little harbour village was a centre for fishing, smuggling and ship building. Today there is a modern wind farm close by and Wylfa nuclear power station a few miles west. The bay's sandy beach and rock pools attract family visitors, and the village makes a fine starting point for cliff walks.

The Tea Shop

Cemaes Heritage Centre with its cosy tea room is located in the middle of the High Street. The varied menu includes salads, jacket potatoes, freshly prepared sandwiches, cream teas, home-made cakes and fruit pies. Crafts and gifts are on sale and the centre can provide you with tourist information. Open Easter to October 9.30am to 5pm. Closed all day Sundays and from 1.30pm on Thursdays. The tea room will open in the winter for groups if they phone in advance to advise the time of arrival. Tel: 01407 711414.

The Walk

1. From the far end of the village car park turn right and pass Victoria Road on the right. Keep ahead to the High Street and cross. (Cemaes Heritage Centre can be seen on the right). Continue

Cemaes harbour

ahead and go down steps into a valley. Go over a footbridge and turn left at a junction. Ignore steps on the right and pass under a bridge. The path bears right to Cemaes harbour.

2. Walk along the sea front with the sea on your left and at the end of the beach keep ahead through a car park to a lane. Shortly turn left on the cliff path. Go up to a kissing gate and follow the path around the headland. You will see Llanbadrig Church above the next bay, Porth Padrig. After going up and down through two small coves, bear right at a fork. Follow a fence on the left to a kissing gate and lane. To visit Llanbadrig Church, turn left.

Llanbadrig Church is the only church in Wales dedicated to St Patrick. According to legend, after being shipwrecked on the tiny island called Middle Mouse, he crossed to Porth Badrig and found refuge in a cave now called Ogof Badrig. In AD 440 he founded his church on this site. The present mediaeval building was restored in the 19th century by Lord Stanley of Alderley (Cheshire). He was a Muslim and the Islam influence is apparent in the stained glass windows. Inside there is the Icthus stone, a standing stone which acquired Christian symbols in the 7ᵗʰ-11ᵗʰ centuries. In 1985 the church was partly burnt down by vandals but afterwards was restored. During the summer it is usually open to visitors during the afternoon.

3. From the church walk back along the lane and keep ahead to a junction. Turn left and follow the lane for about ¾ mile, passing a house called Isallt and a footpath signpost on the right. The lane goes downhill and at a right bend, just before the lane goes uphill, turn left through a kissing gate. The signpost may be hidden in the hedge.

4. Follow the left boundary of the field and cross a track. Continue downhill on a wide path. Go through a kissing gate and keep ahead through a marshy area. At a junction turn left to visit Porth Llanlleina.

Near Porth Llanlleiana is the site of a Christian chapel founded by a female hermit in the 6ᵗʰ or 7ᵗʰ century. The ruined buildings are the remains of a 19ᵗʰ century china clay works where local people processed clay dug from the hillside. It was shipped to porcelain factories from the little harbour.

5. Return along the path and follow it gently uphill. Paths on the left lead to the headland, which is the most northerly point in Wales.

An old watchtower commemorating the coronation of Edward VII (1901) sits on the headland and from here there are extensive views of Anglesey's northern coast. This rocky promontory was the site of Dinas Gynfor, an Iron Age fortress, and its ramparts can be seen on the southern side of the hill.

6. Staying on, or returning to, the lower path, keep ahead. Descend a steep grassy slope into Hell's Mouth and cross an awkward stile. Bear slightly right and follow the path uphill with spectacular views. Care needs to be taken in places at rocky outcrops. The path eventually leads away from the cliffs and descends past some old machinery to a fork. Ignore the path on the left which rises to a mast, and bear right to pass above Porthwen brickworks.

Located close to the sea, Porthwen brickworks is a fascinating indus-

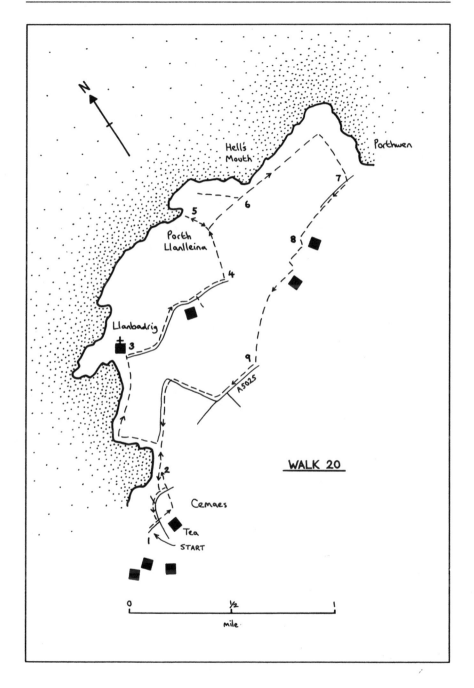

N

Hell's
Mouth

Porthwen

7

6

5

Porth
Llanlleina

8

4

Llanbadrig

3

9

A5025

WALK 20

2

Cemaes

Tea

1   START

0   ½   1
                   mile

trial site with its tall chimneys and beehive shaped kilns. The hill behind provided quartzite for the manufacture of silica bricks which were exported from the quay. However, shipping problems forced the closure of the works in the early 20ᵗʰ century.

7. Go through a kissing gate and follow an enclosed path to a lane. Turn right and in about 300 metres cross a ladder stile on the left. Walk ahead and in a few metres you will have a rocky hillside and a broken wall on the left. Cross a ladder stile and turn left on a track. At the gate to Cae Adda turn right to have a wall on the left.

8. Go around a corner to keep the wall on the left and pass a barn on the right. After passing the barn bear right and continue on a track with a wall on your left. At another wall go through the gap ahead and turn left beside the wall. Before the end of the field bear right and cross a footbridge and stile on the left. Keep ahead to pass farm buildings on the left. Cross the ladder stile ahead and bear right. Cross another stile next to a gate and follow a grassy track through an open field to a ladder stile. Walk beside a wall on the left to another stile then continue beside the wall until you reach a stile at the road.

9. Turn right on the road. There is a grass verge for most of the way. In 300 metres ignore a lane on the left. Continue about another 200 metres and then turn right on a lane signposted Llanbadrig Church. Follow the lane to a junction. Turn left downhill to Cemaes sea front and harbour. At the kiosk bear left uphill to a road. Turn right and shortly bear left to the tea room and starting point.

```
┌─────────────────────────────────────────────┐
│                                               │
│            21. Moelfre                        │
│                                               │
└─────────────────────────────────────────────┘
```

Route: A short but interesting walk. After a stretch of coastal path, the route turns inland to visit prehistoric sites. Some paths could be muddy in the winter.

Distance: 3¾ miles.

How to get there: Leave the A5025 at Llanallgo, north of Benllech. Take the A5108 to Moelfre. After passing shops take the left-hand fork to the car park.

Public Transport: Buses from Bangor and Amlwch.

Start: Signposted car park in the village.

Map: Explorer 263.

The Tea Shop

Formerly a pair of fishermen's cottages, Ann's Pantry is in a lovely position overlooking the cove at Moelfre. There is a tea garden. Breakfasts, light lunches and afternoon teas are served. Soup, salads, jacket potatoes, freshly made sandwiches, bara brith and a variety of delicious home-made cakes are on the menu. Open most of the year but only at weekends in the winter. Hours of opening are 9am-5pm Saturday and Sunday, 11am-5pm weekdays. Tel: 01248 410386.

The Walk

1. Leave the car park by the pedestrian exit and cross the road directly to a footpath. With a stream on your left, pass Ann's Pantry and bear left when you reach a road. On your right is the Hindlea Anchor.

   The anchor is from the Hindlea, a cargo boat, which wrecked off Moelfre on the 27th of October 1959. Moelfre lifeboat rescued all those on board, and the crew received RNLI medals. Shortly after the rescue, the coaster split in two on rocks near the location that the Royal Charter wrecked 100 years earlier.

2. Follow the road as it bears right above the cove. When the road
   bends left, turn right on a short lane which soon narrows into a
   footpath. Pass the Seawatch Centre and the lifeboat station and
   follow the coast path to a shingle beach.

3. At the far end of the beach turn left to continue on the coast path
   above the cliffs. Until recently there was a lookout on this headland. Look across the narrow channel called Y Swnt to Moelfre
   Island. Go through a kissing gate and continue along the grassy
   cliffs, colourful with sea pink and other flowers in late spring
   and early summer. After another kissing gate follow a hedged
   path and enter a caravan site. Walk ahead to meet a track. To
   visit the Royal Charter memorial go through a kissing gate on the
   right. Follow a path downhill and pass above a beach. Go up
   steps and look for a stile on the left which gives access to the memorial.

   The Royal Charter was a fast three masted steam clipper with an iron
   hull. She left Melbourne, Australia on the 20th August 1859 and had almost reached Liverpool, her destination, when she met a north-east
   hurricane force wind as she rounded The Skerries. She dropped anchors,
   but they did not hold and at 3.30 am on the 26th October she split in
   two when she hit rocks near Moelfre. Local people tried to help, but there
   were few survivors, and more than 450 lives were lost. Most of the passengers had been gold diggers returning from Australia's gold fields and
   the ship was carrying gold worth more than £300,000 (a lot of money
   in those days). Looters made their fortunes and Charles Dickens, a
   Times correspondent at that time, came from London and wrote about
   what he witnessed.

4. Return to the caravan site and bear right on the track. Cross a cattle grid and reach a track junction. Bear right to the road. Turn
   right and in 600 metres, after passing Aber Farm on the right,
   turn left at a footpath signpost and kissing gate.

5. Follow the enclosed path into a field. Walk beside the
   right-hand boundary of two fields to a corner stile. Continue beside a left-hand fence around a corner to a ladder stile. Turn
   right on the lane and in about 80 metres bear left through a kissing gate at a signpost for Din Lligwy Ancient village. Follow the

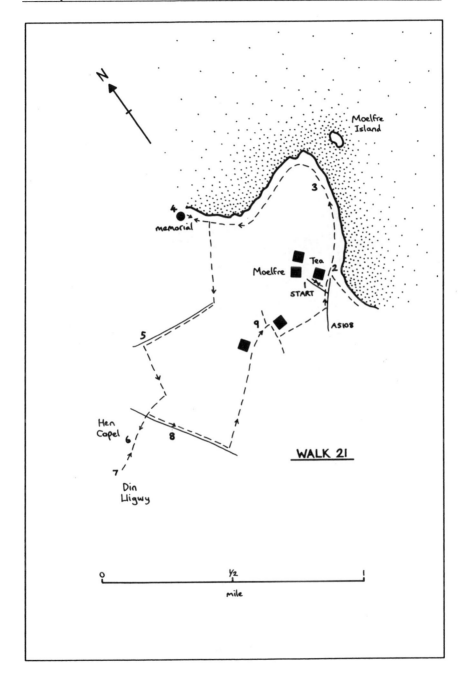

WALK 21

left-hand boundary of the field. Across the field on your right is the ruined chapel called Hen Capel.

Hen (Old) Capel is a small roofless chapel dating back to the 12th century when wooden churches were replaced with stone buildings for the first time. The walls were rebuilt in the 14th century and the south chapel was added in the 16th century. A flight of steps descend to a small crypt.

6. Ignore a gate on the left and slant right across the next field to a kissing gate. Follow the path through the trees to the site of an Iron Age hut group.

Din Lligwy hut circle

Din Lligwy 'village' was probably the home of an important local chieftain in the 4th century AD. Inside the enclosure are two circular huts and several rectangular buildings; they would have been thatched. The circular buildings were used as dwellings, and the others were workshops or barns. Iron smelting hearths, pottery and Roman coins were found during excavations which started in 1905.

7. Walk back through the woodland and fields to the lane. Turn right and in about 200 metres you will see the massive Lligwy burial chamber on your right.

Most of the Lligwy burial chamber lies below ground. Short upright stones support the enormous capstone, which is estimated to weigh about twenty-five tons. Unburned bones of 15-30 people were found when the site was excavated in 1909. Animal bones, flints and Beaker pottery were also present. It is thought the chamber was built in the late Neolithic period.

8. Follow the lane downhill and, just before reaching trees and the bottom of the hill, bear left over a very low stone stile. Follow the right-hand boundary of the field beside a stream. At the end of the field go through a gap in the hedge and walk across the field to a wooden stile. In the next field slant slightly left uphill to the next stile. Maintain your direction to go through a wide gap in some gorse and walk downhill to a corner stile. Follow a hedged path and bear right to buildings.

9. Keep ahead on an access track and go through a gate. At a junction bear right and follow the track to the right of Tyn Coed. Reach a kissing gate and follow an old broken wall on your right. When the wall ends, slant left, descending to the field corner and a path between gorse. In about 50 metres you will reach a fence and then a kissing gate. At the lane turn left over a stream and follow the lane to a road. Turn left, and at a fork bear left to the car park, or right to the tea room. For a short cliff walk before leaving Moelfre, cross steps opposite Ann's Pantry and follow the path past a house onto the cliffs.

22. Benllech

Route: A lovely walk which starts by following the coastal path north, before turning inland through pleasant countryside. Some paths could be muddy in wet weather.

Distance: 5½ miles.

How to get there: Benllech is on the A5025.

Public Transport: Buses from Bangor and Amlwch to the crossroads in Benllech.

Start: Car park opposite Benllech beach.

Map: Explorer 263.

The Tea Shop

Benllech Isaf is a guesthouse and café adjacent to the coastal path at the northern end of Benllech beach. The varied menu includes breakfasts (until 11am) jacket potatoes, sandwiches, scones and home-made cakes. Open Easter to October 8am until late afternoon or early evening. Sundays opens at 10am. Tel: 01248 852700.

The Walk

1. From the car park turn left along the sea front with the sea on your right. Before reaching the entrance to Benllech Isaf, turn right at a footpath signpost. Go down steps and cross some rocks. Climb steps onto the cliffs and continue on the coastal path. It becomes enclosed between hedges then passes a caravan site. Continue through another hedged section and when the path emerges out of the trees, ignore a footpath on the left.

2. Follow the footpath downhill and cross a footbridge over a stream. Do not stray from the path. Go through a kissing gate and at a wooden chalet walk around the headland above Traeth Bychan. After rounding the headland, pass chalets on the left and emerge on a tarmac track. Continue downhill to meet another track coming up from the beach.

Benllech Isaf

3. Turn left on the track to have a stream on the left. When the track bends left through a gate, turn right on an enclosed footpath. In about 60 metres, reach a drive. Keep ahead and shortly turn left through a gate. Follow the track as it bends left and continue to the main road.

4. Cross the road to a track with a footpath signpost. Follow the track in the direction of a farm. When the track bends left at farm buildings, bear right on a path leading to a stone stile beside a stream. Continue along an enclosed path to a field. Walk beside the right boundary of the field and, in a few metres, ignore a stile on the right.

5. Cross a stone stile in the corner of the field and continue along the right edge of small meadows until, shortly before a house, a footpath notice indicates a left turn. Go through a gate on your left and follow the left-hand wall of a garden. Bear right to cross a stream. In another 20 metres look for an arrow on the left and take a path climbing into trees. Follow it to a stone stile and emerge on a lane.

6. Turn left on the lane for 150 metres. Opposite a house called Plas Llanfair turn right over a stone stile. Cross a drive and stile to keep ahead between trees. Cross two stiles and turn left to another stile. Bear slightly right and go through a long gate. Continue with a fence on the right and climb steps to the left of the next gate. Keep ahead through a long field. Look for a stone stile about 25 metres left of the right corner. Cross stones in a small stream and another stile. Follow the left-hand hedge and ignore an enclosed path on the left.

7. Cross a stone stile and immediately bear right to a narrow stile in a wall. Walk beside the right-hand hedge to stone steps and a little gate. Bear left and follow a wall on the right to an access drive coming from a house. Cross a stile near a gate and note the kissing gate on the left. To see Llanfair Mathafarn Eithaf Church continue along the drive and turn left on the lane.

Llanfair Mathafarn Eithaf Church has an 11th century cross in the churchyard. The 18th century Welsh poet Goronwy Owen was born in this parish and for a few weeks was curate of this church. He later sailed to Virginia in America and eventually became the owner of a cotton and tobacco plantation. One of his greatest poems was called Cywydd Hiraeth am Fon (Longing for Anglesey). George Borrow visited the hamlet in 1854 whilst touring Wales.

8. Return to the kissing gate on the drive and follow a clear path downhill. Cross a stream and continue beside the left-hand wall to a stone stile. The path becomes enclosed and goes through a kissing gate. Emerge on a drive coming from Ty Mawr and follow it to a road.

9. Cross the road and turn right. In about 50 metres bear left up steps. Walk along an embankment to a field. Turn right and follow the right-hand hedge to a stile near a gate. Walk across the middle of the field bearing slightly left. To the right of the far left corner, cross a stile. Keep ahead on a path through gorse. When you reach open space continue ahead to Pant y Saer burial chamber.

Excavations at Pant y Saer Neolithic burial chamber have revealed the bones of fifty-four persons, including children. The tomb was probably in use over a long period of time.

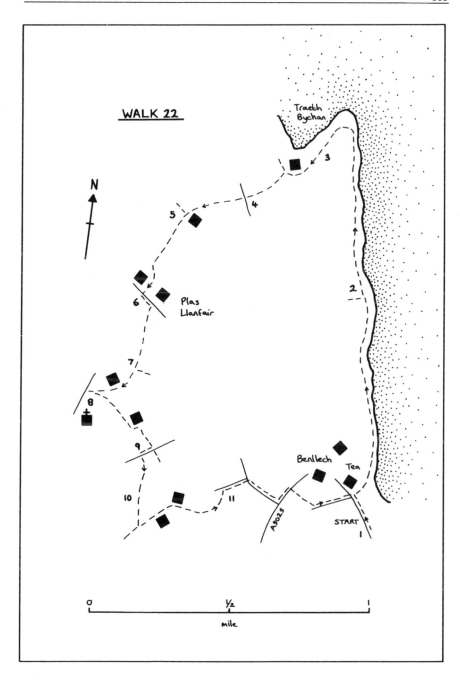

WALK 22

N

Traeth Bychan

3

4

5

6 Plas Llanfair

2

7

8

9

10

11

Benllech Tea

A.5025

START

1

0 ½ 1

mile

10. Bear left at the burial chamber, and shortly slant right on a path through gorse. The path bears right to descend into a lower field. Turn left to follow the left boundary to a kissing gate. Turn left on a track and pass some houses. At a fork turn right on the drive to Ty Gwyn. When the track bends left, keep ahead on a path beside a fence. It rises to a kissing gate. The path shortly bears left through trees and gorse to another gate. Continue around bends to a road.

11. Bear right downhill and at a junction turn right to the main road, the A5025. Cross and turn left. In about 60 metres bear right on a path beside a stream. Go through a kissing gate and cross a parking area. Cross a road and follow a path beside a wall and fence. At a road, turn left downhill and emerge near the sea front opposite Benllech Isaf Café.

23. Red Wharf Bay

Route: This varied walk crosses Benllech Sand then turns inland through lovely countryside. The beach may be impassable at high tide so start the walk when the sea is going out or at low tide.

Distance: 6 miles.

How to get there: Leave the A5025 north of Pentraeth on a road signposted Red Wharf Bay (Traeth Coch).

Public Transport: Buses from Bangor and Amlwch to the village, ½ mile from the start.

Start: Car park along the sea front at Red Wharf Bay.

Map: Explorer 263.

A quiet place nowadays, in the 19th century Red Wharf Bay had a busy shipyard and a working limestone quarry. If you venture onto

Red Wharf Bay

the sand beware the incoming tide, which swiftly floods the channels and pools. There is a legend that a boat full of red-haired witches landed on the sands of Red Wharf Bay and settled in Llanddona, on the east side of the bay. They became famous for their spells and curses and it was said the men could blind people. It is probable that they were shipwreck victims and local people were afraid of them because they spoke a foreign language.

The Tea Shop

Near the sea front at Red Wharf Bay is The Old Boathouse Café and Restaurant with its tea garden, a popular refreshment stop for walkers. The menu includes jacket potatoes, freshly prepared and toasted sandwiches, home-made scones and a scrumptious selection of cakes. Open all day 10am-9pm, every day, but closes on Mondays and Tuesdays in the winter. Tel: 01248 852731.

The Walk

1. From the parking area, walk back towards the road out of the bay. Do not go uphill but walk ahead with the bay on your right. Pass Min y Don Hotel on the left and a house on the right. Shortly after passing a garage on the left, turn left on a path. It goes uphill and bears right before reaching a caravan site.

2. Pass the caravan site on your left. When the path reaches a track, where there is a gate on the right, turn left on the track to a junction. Turn right along the site access drive, but in about 20 metres turn left on a narrow path. It passes through trees parallel to the drive. In 200 metres you will reach a wide track on the left. Follow this track uphill for about 40 metres then bear right on a path. Go through some trees and, after passing the clubhouse, bear left to the beach.

3. Turn left along Benllech Sand. Join a road at Wendon Café near a car park. Go through the car park and up some steps to a fence. Bear right beside the fence and follow the path when it bends left. Ignore a path on the right. Walk away from the sea to a kissing gate and turn left along the road. Continue uphill along Bay View Road.

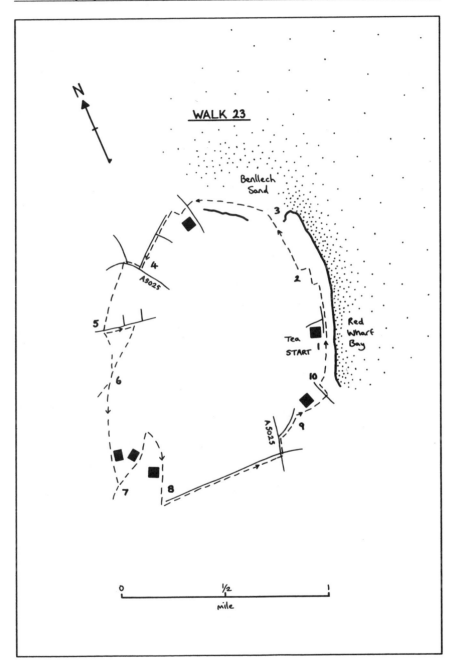

N

WALK 23

Benllech Sand

3

2

A5025

4

5

Tea
START 1

Red
Wharf
Bay

10

6

9

A5025

7 8

0   ½   1
          mile

4. At the junction with the A5025 turn right for about 150 metres and before reaching the Plas Glanrafon Hotel turn left on a road. In a few metres, where the road bends right, turn left through a kissing gate. Follow a stream on the right. The path eventually goes up steps and passes behind gardens then enters a field. Keep ahead to another field. Continue ahead but bear slightly right to a stone stile near a gate in the right-hand corner of the field.

5. Turn left on the lane and ignore a path on the right. Pass a road on the left (Upper Breeze Hill) and in a few paces, near the next road on the left, turn right on an enclosed footpath. In 600 metres pass a kissing gate on the right, and in a few more metres turn left through a kissing gate.

6. Follow a clear path through low gorse in the direction of a wooded hill. When the path reaches the corner of a small gorse enclosed field, bear left through bushes and walk across this field to a path going uphill. Climb up through trees and bushes to a ladder stile. Walk along the right side of a field and at the far end bear left in the direction of a house. Go through a kissing gate to the right of the house. Cross the next field by bearing slightly right to another kissing gate. Turn right on an access drive.

7. At a junction with another drive, bear left. In about 80 metres, at the entrance gate to the house, turn right through a gate. Bear diagonally left across the field to a kissing gate. In the next field turn left to follow the boundary to a kissing gate in the far corner. Now bear left around the side of the field. Continue along the top of the field to where a track joins on the left. Here turn right downhill, passing opposite the kissing gate by which you entered the field. The path enters trees and goes up steps to a kissing gate. Follow the right boundary of this field to a stone stile next to a field gate. Turn left along the drive and follow it to a lane.

8. Turn left along the lane for ¾ mile to the A5025. Turn left and in 100 metres bear right on the road signposted Red Wharf Bay (Traeth Coch).

9. In 200 metres turn right along the drive to Banc y Ffynnon Mawr

and Banc y Ffynnon Bach. Before reaching Banc y Ffynnon Mawr, bear right to follow a path outside the garden fence. It passes alongside a number of gardens and crosses a footbridge over a stream. It eventually bears right and emerges on a lane.

10. Turn left and in 40 metres go through a kissing gate on your right. Follow a path through a field to another kissing gate. Continue beside a fence and above houses. Go through a kissing gate and pass through trees. The path descends to The Ship Inn at Red Wharf Bay. Continue ahead to the parking area and The Old Boathouse Restaurant and Café.

---

24. Penmon Point

Route: A short but interesting walk with beautiful views in the historic eastern corner of Anglesey.

Distance: 3 miles.

How to get there: From Beaumaris take the B5109 for 1½ miles. At a crossroads turn right and at the next junction turn right again. From the church follow the toll road to Penmon Point. A charge is made for all vehicles using the road.

Public Transport: Buses from Bangor and Beaumaris to Penmon, ½ mile off route (Direction 4).

Start: Parking area near the end of the toll road at Penmon Point (Trwyn Du).

Map: Explorer 263.

From Penmon Point there are superb views of Puffin Island, the Great Orme and Snowdonia. A channel 800 metres wide separates the mainland of Anglesey from Puffin Island. Other names for the uninhabited island include Ynys Seirol, Ynys Glannauc, Ynys Lannog and Priestholm. St Seirol founded a sanctuary there in the sixth century and the island is believed to be his burial place. The ruins of a 12th century church may be glimpsed from above Penmon Point. Another ruin on the island is the 19th century semaphore station, one of a chain which linked Holyhead to Liverpool. Gulls, cormorants, guillemots and puffins nest on the island. The population of puffins has dwindled. Rats may be the cause of their decline, but in the 19th century puffins were caught, pickled and exported in barrels as a delicacy.

Shrews, voles. hedgehogs, stonechats, merlins and other birds of prey may be spotted on the headland at Penmon Point. In spring and early summer look for butterflies such as the peacock and common blue.

The Tea Shop

Built in the 1850s, the Pilot House Café was formerly three pilot cottages. There is also seating outside. Jacket potatoes, sandwiches and a good selection of cakes are on offer. Open Easter until the end of September. Early and late season, 12 noon-4pm; at other times 11am-5pm. In bad weather it is advisable to phone beforehand to check the café is open. Large groups are also asked to phone in advance of their arrival. Tel: 01248 490206

Penmon

The Walk

1. From the road near Pilot House Café and with your back to Puffin Island, look for a path on the right. Pass a waymarked post and follow the path uphill through bracken and small trees to a ladder stile. Walk ahead to a track and turn right. Cross a stile on the left and continue ahead, beside a hedge. Before reaching a gate, climb a stone stile on the right. Bear left to pass the gate and follow a high wall on your left.

A deer park was established at Penmon after the dissolution of the monasteries. The Bulkeley family built several miles of these high walls to retain the animals, but no deer have been here since the early years of the 20th century.

2. Cross a stone stile in the left corner of the field. Continue ahead beside the wall, towards a cottage. Ignore a kissing gate on the left and pass the cottage on your right. Go through the kissing gate ahead. Walk along the lane, passing a few houses.

3. At a junction with another lane, turn left. After passing a large white house on the left called Dinmor, the lane starts to go downhill. Near a gate on the left look for some steps.

4. Climb the steps to a small gate and walk ahead through the field in the direction of the Great Orme. In about 300 metres there will be rocky outcrops on your left. Walk on towards the Great Orme but head closer to the rocky hillside. When Penmon Church, dovecote and other buildings are in view, look for a track on the left. Follow it downhill and ignore other tracks off it. When you reach a gate, do not go through it. Bear left, in about 70 metres, go up some steps in the wall and follow a path to the road. Turn left to Penmon Priory, the church, dovecote and St Seirol's Well.

St Seirol founded a religious community at Penmon in the sixth century. Vikings destroyed the original church in AD 971 and it was replaced by the present building in the 12th century. The monks joined the Augustinian order in the following century. After the Dissolution of the Monasteries about 1537, the buildings and land passed to the Bulkeley family of Baron Hill, Beaumaris. The ruined monastery walls consist of the monks' refectory and kitchen, which had a dormitory above and cellars underneath. The 12th century church is the most complete of its period on Anglesey. Its chancel was added in the 13th century but rebuilt in 1855. Inside are two elaborate Celtic crosses which once stood in the enclosure of the medieval monastery. The larger cross was in the deer park until it was brought into the church for protection. To the right is the remarkable dovecote built about AD 1600 by Sir Richard Bulkeley. The little building housed about 1000 pigeons. Their eggs were collected from the nesting holes by placing a ladder on the central pillar. A path opposite the dovecote leads to St Seirol's Well, the monastery's water supply. At one time this holy well was reputed to have healing powers and the brick structure around the pool dates from the 18th century. According to legend, St Seirol lived in a cell below the nearby cliff. A

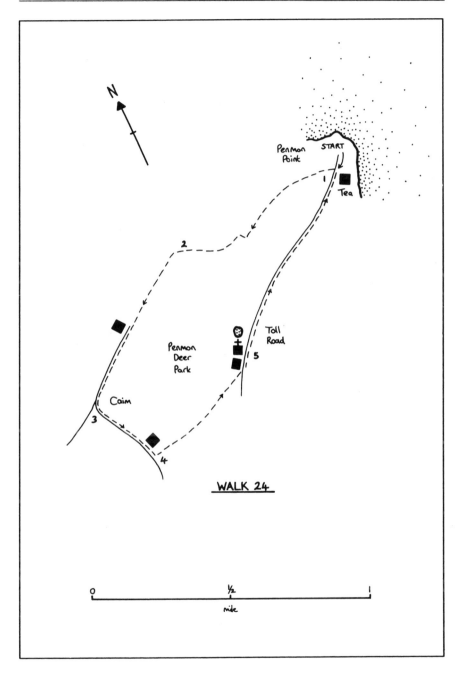

N

Penmon
Point   START

1

Tea

2

Toll
Road

Penmon
Deer
Park   5

Caim

3

4

WALK 24

0   ½   1
            mile

story about the saint relates how once a week he used to cross the island to meet his friend St Cybi (of Holyhead) at springs near Llannerch-y-medd. St Cybi walked facing the sun in the morning and again in the evening so he became sun-tanned and was called Cybi the Dark. St Seirol having the sun behind him all day remained pale and was known as Seirol the Fair.

5. Follow the road to the parking area and café.

25. Beaumaris

Route: The length of this walk depends on the state of the tide. The longer route involves 1½ miles of beach walking which must only be attempted at low tide or when the sea is going out. However, in suitable conditions this is a lovely walk with fine views across the Menai Strait.

Distance: 2¼ or 5¾ miles.

How to get there: From Menai Bridge follow the A545 to Beaumaris.

Public Transport: Buses from Bangor and Menai Bridge.

Start: Car park on The Green near the castle in Beaumaris.

Map: Explorer 263.

The town of Beaumaris dates from the 13th century when Edward I was completing his programme of castle building in North Wales. The Norman French name reflects the chosen site: 'beau mareys'

Beaumaris Castle

means beautiful marsh. The low-lying flat ground enabled the Savoyard architect Master James of St George to achieve a symmetrical design, but money ran out and the castle was never completed. The town was built at the same time and received its charter in 1296. For many centuries Beaumaris was the most important town on Anglesey.

The Tea Shop

The Spinning Wheel Tea Room is in a Georgian building situated near the castle. Sandwiches, bara brith, Welsh cakes, cream teas and a selection of home-made cakes are on offer. Light lunches are also available. Open most of the year (check in the winter) every day from 10am-4.30pm, sometimes later in the summer. Tel: 01248 810338.

The Walk

1. From the car park on The Green walk along the sea front with the Menai Strait on your right. At the entrance gate to Beaumaris Marine World go through a kissing gate on the left. Follow the path along the cliff, soon having fine views of the island's coastline, and Snowdonia across the strait. Descend to a kissing gate and continue along the pavement. When the pavement ends, keep ahead along the back of the beach and cross a stream near some trees.

2. **Warning** – only continue with the longer walk if the tide is low or going out.
   If the tidal conditions are not suitable for continuing along the beach, walk back along the road for about 100 metres and turn right on a road. Ignore a lane on the left and keep ahead another 300 metres to Llanfaes Lodge. In front of the lodge turn left through a small gate, where you join the longer route (Direction 8).
   If the tide is low or going out, continue along the shingle beach. Pass some houses and, further on, some crumbling cliffs. After walking along the beach for nearly 1½ miles, you will reach the River Lleiniog.

3. Turn inland with the river on your right and follow a path to a road. Turn left and, just beyond a left bend, turn right on a track.

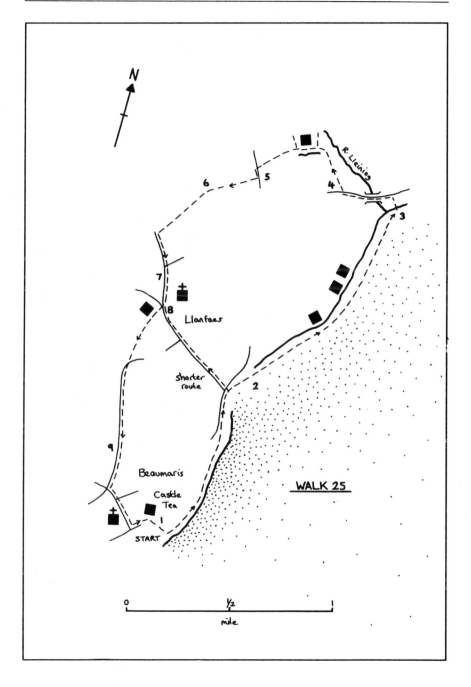

WALK 25

It narrows into a path and goes through a kissing gate. Continue through woodland. Trees on the right conceal the remains of Aberlleiniog Castle.

The Normans built a motte and bailey on the opposite side of Afon Lleiniog. In 1094, Gruffudd ap Cynan won the castle for the Welsh at the Battle of Aberlleiniog. The Earl of Chester, Hugh d'Avranches, was killed by an arrow in the eye. In the 17th century a small stone castle was built on the site. It is now a ruin.

4. Go through another kissing gate. The path joins a track coming from the waterworks. Walk ahead and, after crossing a bridge over a stream, turn left on a path. Pass a house on the right. The path becomes clearer and shortly enclosed between bushes and a banking. Go through a gate and turn left. Follow the path past gardens and through woodland to the road in Llangoed.

5. Turn left and in about 100 metres turn right at a footpath sign-post. Go through a gate and follow a path along the left side of a field to a corner stile. Keep ahead through a caravan site. You will pass a post with a yellow arrow. Follow a track to the left. When you reach another waymarked post, turn right on a track to another post near a tap. Walk between caravans to find a ladder stile behind the right-hand caravan.

6. Cross the middle of a field, slanting slightly left towards the tall Bulkeley monument seen on the skyline. Look for a post with a yellow arrow on it, and cross a plank bridge and stone stile. In the next field, continue towards the monument. Cross a ladder stile near a gate and turn left uphill on a lane. Ignore a lane on the left and go downhill, passing cottages and the track leading to Llanfaes Church.

Llanfaes was an important trading centre before the English invasion. Llywelyn the Great founded a Franciscan friary not far from the strait and it was the burial place of his wife Siwan, Princess Joan, daughter of King John. Her coffin can be seen in Beaumaris Church. When Edward I built his castle at Beaumaris, the inhabitants of Llanfaes were evicted to a 'new borough' near Rhosyr, now known as Newborough.

7. At a lane junction turn left and, after passing the gate to Llanfaes Lodge, turn right through a small gate.

8. Follow a short section of enclosed path to a small gate. Keep ahead through a golf course. You will pass a yellow arrow on a post. On reaching a fence corner, continue ahead with the fence on your left. Go through a kissing gate and turn right on a lane. Follow the lane as it bends to the left. The derelict mansion Baron Hill stands on the wooded hill to your right.

The locally important Bulkeley family built the first Baron Hill mansion in 1618. William Bulkeley of Cheshire was made Constable of the Castle in 1440 and the tomb belonging to him and his wife, Elen, is in Beaumaris Church. The tall monument seen on the walk was erected in honour of Sir Richard Williams Bulkeley who died in 1875. The Baron Hill mansion was rebuilt several times and in the Second World War it was a military hospital.

9. Further along the lane, Beaumaris Castle is in view across a field on the left. When the lane emerges on a road, turn left. Pass the church of St Mary and St Nicholas on the right. At the main road turn left to the castle, tea room and car park.

Tea Shop Walks - Spreading everywhere!

The Sigma Leisure Tea Shop Walks series already includes:

Cheshire

The Chilterns

The Clwydian Hills & Welsh Borderlands

The Cotswolds

The Lake District, Volume 1

The Lake District, Volume 2

Lancashire

Leicestershire & Rutland

North Devon

The Peak District

Shropshire

Snowdonia

South Devon

Staffordshire

Surrey & Sussex

Warwickshire

The Yorkshire Dales

Each book costs £6.95 and contains an average of 25 excellent walks: far better value than any other competitor!

DISCOVERY WALKS IN NORTH WALES
Anna & Graham Francis
21 routes to sites of particular beauty or interest, from leisurely strolls of a couple of miles to more arduous 8-mile rambles. The book explores imposing castles, spectacular waterfalls, copper mines and steam railways. Anna Francis provides pen and ink drawings and there is also an aerial picture map for each route. £6.95

OFFA'S DYKE CIRCULAR WALKS (Two volumes - Northern and Southern Sections)
Ian Coulthard
Each book contains 25 energetic and challenging circular hill walks based on Offa's Dyke National Trail. Walks range from 5 to 13 miles (3 to 7 hours), and concise instructions include height gain, local facilities and summaries of terrain and ground conditions. Sketch maps are to scale – a boon in this demanding terrain. Suggested starting points give the more demanding elements in the first few miles. £7.95 per volume

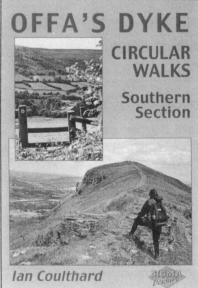

In case of difficulty, or for a free catalogue, please contact:
SIGMA LEISURE, 1 SOUTH OAK LANE, WILMSLOW, CHESHIRE SK9 6AR.
Phone: 01625-531035
Fax: 01625-536800.
E-mail: info@sigmapress.co.uk
Web site: http//www.sigmapress.co.uk

VISA and MASTERCARD orders welcome.